Fun & Original
Character
Cakes

Fun & Original
Character Cakes

Maisie Parrish

David and Charles

www.mycraftivity.com

A DAVID & CHARLES BOOK
Copyright © David & Charles Limited 2009

David & Charles is an F+W Media Inc. company
4700 East Galbraith Road,
Cincinnati, OH 45236

First published in the UK in 2009

Text and designs copyright © Maisie Parrish 2009
Photography copyright © David & Charles 2009

A catalogue record for this book is available from the British Library.

ISBN-13: 978-0-7153-3005-0 paperback
ISBN-10: 0-7153-3005-5 paperback

Printed in China by ShenZhen Donnelley Printing Co. Ltd.
for David & Charles
Brunel House   Newton Abbot   Devon

Commissioning Editor: Jennifer Fox-Proverbs
Editor: Bethany Dymond
Project Editor: Ame Verso
Art Editors: Sarah Underhill and Charly Bailey
Designer: Mia Farrant
Production Controller: Kelly Smith
Photographers: Karl Adamson and Simon Whitmore

Visit our website at www.davidandcharles.co.uk

David & Charles books are available from all good bookshops; alternatively you can contact our Orderline on 0870 9908222 or write to us at FREEPOST EX2 110, D&C Direct, Newton Abbot, TQ12 4ZZ (no stamp required UK only); US customers call 800-289-0963 and Canadian customers call 800-840-5220.

I dedicate this book to the memory of my daughter *Julie Ann*, a passionate lover of animals, and to my grandchildren *Samantha, Rebecca* and *Jessica*.

IMPORTANT NOTE
The models in this book were made using metric measurements. Imperial conversions have been provided, but the reader is advised that these are approximate and therefore significantly less precise than using the metric measurements given. By means of example, using metric a quantity of 1g can easily be measured, whereas the smallest quantity given in imperial on most modern electric scales is $\frac{1}{8}$oz. The author and publisher cannot therefore be held responsible for any errors incurred by using the imperial measurements in this book and advise the reader to use the metric equivalents wherever possible.

Contents

Introduction

If you are just starting out in the novelty cake-decorating world, this is the book for you! It has all the advice you need, with clear step-by-step photographs to guide you through each cake project. On these pages you can discover and enjoy eight new ideas for novelty cakes including over 30 individual characters – explained in simple terms – all using the same fundamental techniques.

Novelty cake decorating is a very happy experience, full of colour and fun, with characters to delight all ages. Whether you copy my cakes to the letter, or use them as a springboard for your own designs, I am sure you will find something here to inspire you to get creative in the kitchen.

Those of you who are familiar with my work will know that I often feature animals on my cakes. This collection takes the animal theme one step further, giving you creatures bursting with character for all occasions, which I am certain you will have fun making. From chocoholic bunnies to carol-singing penguins and newly-wed cats – there are brightly coloured animal-themed cakes here for all the major celebrations in life, all of which are guaranteed to be conversation pieces at any party. And if you are short of time to make an entire cake, it's so simple to select your favourite characters and apply them to a pre-bought cake for quick and stunning results.

You will find my techniques are basic and simple to achieve, so when you have mastered them, you can elaborate with as much detail as you like. All the models start from a simple ball and grow and develop from there in many different ways. But the most important thing is that I have tried to show you how to put humour, movement and life into your work, which is the key to the success of these cakes.

Take the time to read the book carefully before you start and make sure you have all the equipment you need for things to go smoothly. And remember ... everything starts with a ball!

Enjoy,

Maisie

Sugarpaste

All the models in this book are made using sugarpaste (rolled fondant) in one form or another. This firm, sweet paste is also used to cover cakes and boards. Sugarpaste is very soft and pliable and marks very easily, but for modelling it works best if you add CMC (Tylose) or gum tragacanth to it to bulk it up (see Sugarpaste for Modelling, opposite). This section gives you the lowdown on this wonderful medium, revealing everything you need to know for success with sugarpaste.

Ready-Made Sugarpaste

You can purchase sugarpaste in the most amazing array of colours; just take it out of the packet and away you go. Of all the ready-made pastes on the market, the brand leader is Renshaws Regalice (see Suppliers, page 126), which is available in white and 14 other exciting shades. This paste is easy to work with and is of excellent firm quality.

Tip

Very dark colours, such as black, dark blue and brown, are particularly useful to buy ready-coloured, because if you add enough paste food colouring into white to obtain a strong shade, it will alter the consistency of the paste and make it much more difficult to work with.

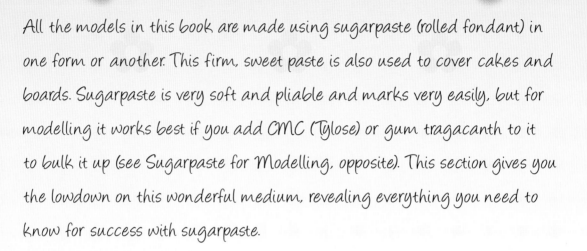

Ready-made packaged sugarpaste is quick and convenient to use. Well-known brands are high quality and give consistently good results.

Making Your Own

While the ready-made sugarpaste is excellent, you can, of course, make your own at home. The bonus of this is that you can then tint your paste to any colour you like using edible paste food colour (see page 10). This can then be dusted with edible dust food colour to intensify or soften the shade.

Sugarpaste Recipe

* 900g (2lb) sifted icing (confectioners') sugar
* 120ml (8tbsp) liquid glucose
* 15g (½oz) gelatin
* 15ml (1tbsp) glycerine
* 45ml (3tbsp) cold water

1 Sprinkle the gelatin over the cold water and allow to 'sponge'. Place over a bowl of hot water and stir with a wooden spoon until all the gelatin crystals have dissolved. Do not allow the gelatin mixture to boil.

2 Add the glycerine and glucose to the gelatin and stir until melted.

3 Add the liquid mixture to the sifted icing (confectioners') sugar and mix thoroughly until combined.

4 Dust the work surface lightly with icing (confectioners') sugar, then turn out the paste and knead to a soft consistency until smooth and free of cracks.

5 Wrap the sugarpaste completely in cling film or store in an airtight polythene bag. If the paste is too soft and sticky to handle, work in a little more icing (confectioners') sugar.

Quick Sugarpaste Recipe

* 500g (1lb 1½oz) sifted icing (confectioners') sugar
* 1 egg white
* 30ml (2tbsp) liquid glucose

1 Place the egg white and liquid glucose in a clean bowl. Add the icing (confectioners') sugar and mix together with a wooden spoon, then use your hands to bring the mixture into a ball.

2 Follow steps 4 and 5 of the above recipe for kneading and storage.

Sugarpaste is such a versatile modelling medium, it can be used to create an almost endless variety of cute characters.

Sugarpaste for Modelling

To convert sugarpaste into modelling paste, all you need to do is add CMC (Tylose) powder or gum tragacanth (see page 25) to the basic recipe. The quantity needed will vary according to the temperature and humidity of the room, so you may need to experiment to get the right mix depending on the conditions you are working in. As a guide, add roughly 5ml (1tsp) of gum tragacanth or CMC (Tylose) to 225g (8oz) of sugarpaste and knead well. Place inside a polythene bag and allow the CMC/gum to do its work for at least two hours. Knead the paste before use to warm it up with your hands; this will make it more pliable and easier to use.

Throughout this book I have used the combination of sugarpaste and CMC (Tylose) powder, and find it works very well. I personally prefer it to gum tragacanth. If you do add too much CMC (Tylose) to the paste it will begin to crack, which is not desirable. Should this happen, add a little white vegetable fat (shortening) to soften it and make it pliable again.

Colouring Sugarpaste

Whether you choose to make your own, or to buy ready-made sugarpaste, the white variety of both forms can be coloured with paste food colourings to provide a wonderful spectrum of colours.

Solid Colours

1 Roll the sugarpaste to be coloured into a smooth ball and run your palm over the top. Take a cocktail stick or toothpick and dip it into the paste food colour. Apply the colour over the surface of the sugarpaste. Do not add too much at first, as you can always add more if required.

2 Dip your finger into some cool boiled water, shaking off any excess and run it over the top of the colour. This will allow the colour to disperse much more quickly into the sugarpaste.

3 Dust the work surface with icing (confectioners') sugar and knead the colour evenly into the paste.

4 The colour will deepen slightly as it stands. If you want to darken it even more, just add more paste colour and knead again.

Marbled Effect

1 Apply the paste food colour to the sugarpaste as directed above, but instead of working it until the colour is evenly dispersed, knead it for a shorter time to give a marbled effect.

2 You can also marble two or more colours into a sausage shape, twist them together and then roll into a ball. Again, do not blend them together too much. Cakes and boards look particularly nice when covered with marbled paste.

Tip

When colouring white sugarpaste, do not use liquid food colour as it will make the paste too sticky.

Edible food colours come in a wide variety of forms – liquid, paste, dust and even pens – all of which can be used to add colour and life to your sugarpaste models.

Painting on Sugarpaste

There are various different ways of painting on to sugarpaste. The most common way is to use paste food colour diluted with some cooled boiled water, or you can use liquid food colours and gels. There are also some food colour pens available, but these tend to work better on harder surfaces. Another way is to dilute dust food colour with clear alcohol; this is particularly useful if you want it to dry quickly. Just wash your paintbrush in clean water when you have finished.

Brushes

In terms of brushes, to paint facial features I use No.00 or 000 sable paintbrushes. The finer and better quality the brush the better job you will make of it. To dust the cheeks of my figures I use a cosmetics brush, which has a sponge at one end and a brush at the other. For more detailed work, you can use a variety of sable brushes in different widths.

The cheeks of this hippo were dusted with pink dust food colour and a cosmetics brush to give her a nice healthy glow.

Storing Sugarpaste

Sugarpaste will always store best wrapped tightly in a polythene bag, making sure you have removed as much air as possible, and then placed in an airtight container to protect it from atmospheric changes. It should be kept out of the sunlight and away from any humidity, in a cool, dry area at least half a metre (20in) off the ground. If the paste has become too dry to work with, knead in some white vegetable fat (shortening). The main thing to remember with any paste is to keep it dry, cool and sealed from the air, as this will make it dry out and go hard.

Food colour pens can be used to add quick and simple embellishments, such as the red dots on this bear's dress. They are cleaner and easier to use than liquid food colours.

For a quick effect, eyelashes can be painted on with liquid food colour and a No.00 paintbrush to really bring the character's expression to life.

Modelling

Mastering modelling with sugarpaste is the key to creating professional-looking cakes. This section reveals all the tools and techniques you need to help sharpen your modelling skills.

General Equipment

There is a myriad of tools on the market for cake decorating and sugarcraft, but many of them are simply unnecessary. The following list gives my recommended essentials, and these are the items that form the basic tool kit listed in each of the projects in this book.

⭐ **Large non-stick rolling pin**

For rolling out sugarpaste and marzipan.

⭐ **Wooden spacing rods (1)**

For achieving an even thickness when rolling out sugarpaste – available in various thicknesses.

⭐ **Two cake smoothers with handles (2)**

For smoothing sugarpaste when covering cakes – use two together for a professional finish.

⭐ **Flower former (3)**

For placing delicate parts in while working on them so that they do not lose their shape.

⭐ **Paint palette (4)**

For mixing liquid food colour or dust food colour and clear alcohol in for painting on to sugarpaste.

⭐ **Quality sable paintbrushes (5)**

For painting on to sugarpaste and for modelling – used mainly for painting facial features, applying edible glue and adding paste. The end of a paintbrush can be pushed into models to create nostrils, used to curl laces of paste around to make curly tails or hair, and used to open up flower petals.

⭐ **Textured rolling pins (6)**

For creating decorative patterns in pieces of sugarpaste – for example, rice textured, daisy patterned and ribbed.

⭐ **Pastry brush (7)**

For smoothing on glaze or buttercream.

⭐ **Cutting wheel (8)**

For making smooth cuts on long pieces of sugarpaste, for use on borders mainly. A pizza cutter can be used instead.

(9)

(8)

(10)

(7)

★ **Plastic marzipan knife**

For trimming the edges of cakes and boards for a neat result.

★ **Sugar press (9)**

For extruding lengths of paste to make grass, wool, fluff and hair – a standard garlic press, found in all kitchens, is very effective for this.

★ **Plunger cutters (10)**

For cutting out different shapes in sugarpaste – such as daisies, hearts, stars and flowers.

★ **Good-quality stainless steel cutters**

Round, square, rectangle, butterfly, heart, petal/blossom – in assorted sizes. For cutting out clean shapes for use in decorations.

★ **Frilling tool**

For making frills in sugar flower paste pieces – a cocktail stick or toothpick can be used instead.

★ **Cake cards**

For placing models on while working on them before transferring them to the cake.

★ **Mini turntable (11)**

Useful for placing a cake on so that it can be easily turned around while working on it – not essential.

★ **Measuring cups (12)**

For measuring out powders and liquids quickly and cleanly.

★ **Flower stamens (13)**

For creating whiskers or antennae on sugarpaste animals and insects.

★ **Non-stick flexi mat**

For placing over modelled parts to prevent them from drying out – polythene bags can be used instead.

★ **Cake boards (14)**

For placing cakes on prior to covering with sugarpaste for a professional-looking result.

(11) **(12)** **(13)** **(14)**

Specific Modelling Tools

A whole book could be filled talking about these, as there are so many different varieties available. However, I use the white plastic set that has a number on each tool. I refer to the number on the tool throughout the book. They are inexpensive, light and easy to work with, and are available to buy from my website (see Suppliers, page 126).

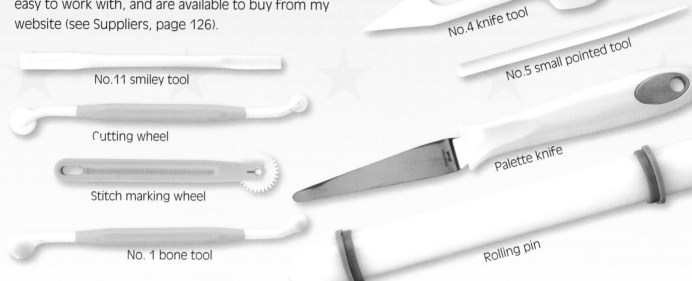

No.12 stitch marking tool

No.3 tapered cone/ball tool

No.4 knife tool

No.5 small pointed tool

No.11 smiley tool

Cutting wheel

Palette knife

Stitch marking wheel

No. 1 bone tool

Rolling pin

Securing and Supporting Your Models

Sugarpaste models need to be held together in several ways. Small parts can be attached with edible glue (see page 23), but larger parts, such as heads and arms, will require additional support.

Throughout the book I use pieces of dry spaghetti for this purpose. The spaghetti is inserted into the models – into the hip, shoulder or body, for example – leaving approximately 2cm (¾in) on to which you can attach another piece – the leg, arm or head. The pieces will still require some edible glue to bond them, but will have more support and will stay rigid. When inserting spaghetti to support heads, make sure that it is pushed into the body in a very vertical position otherwise the head will tilt backwards and become vulnerable. Spaghetti can also be used for weaving around to make baskets, such as in the Easter Bunnies cake on page 34.

I recommend using dry spaghetti because it is food and is much safer than using cocktail sticks or toothpicks, which could cause harm, particularly to children. However, I would always advise that the spaghetti is removed before eating the cake and decorations. If you would prefer to use pastillage sugar sticks instead, you can find the recipe for these on page 22 – but these should also to be removed prior to eating.

Sugarpaste models sometimes need to be supported with foam or cardboard while they are drying to prevent parts from flopping over or drooping down. Advice on where this may be necessary is given in the project instructions.

Basic Shapes

There are four basic shapes required for modelling. Every character in this book begins with a ball; this shape must be rolled first, regardless of whatever shape you are trying to make.

Ball

The first step is always to roll a ball. We do this to ensure that we have a perfectly smooth surface, with no cracks or creases.

For example:

If you pull out the ball at the front, you can shape it into an animal's face.

Sausage

From this shape we can make arms and legs. It is simple to make by applying even pressure to the ball and continuing to roll, keeping it uniform thickness along its length.

For example:

The sausage shape when turned up at the end will form a foot, or can be marked to make a paw.

Cone

This shape is the basis for all bodies. It is made by rolling and narrowing the ball at one end, leaving it fatter at the other.

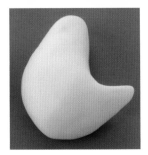

For example:

The cone can be pulled out at the widest part to form the body of a bird.

Oval

This is the least used of the basic shapes, but is used to make cheeks, ears and other small parts. It is made in the same way as the sausage, by applying even pressure to the ball, but not taking it as far.

For example:

Smaller oval shapes can be used for ears.

Creating Animal Characters

Using the basic shapes as a starting point, you can create a vast selection of different animals full of personality and charm. Each project gives detailed instructions for creating the featured characters, but here is a sample of some additional animals with advice on how to model them. Use these examples to practise and hone your modelling skills before you launch into the cake projects.

Mouse

Mice are well known for causing trouble and can be great characters to have on a cake. They come in many sizes and shapes, but all have shared characteristics. The shorter the nose the cuter the mouse will look; if it gets too long it will start to look more like a rat. Three basic shapes are needed: ball, cone and oval.

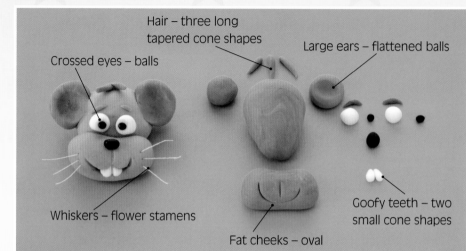

Hair – three long tapered cone shapes

Crossed eyes – balls

Large ears – flattened balls

Whiskers – flower stamens

Goofy teeth – two small cone shapes

Fat cheeks – oval

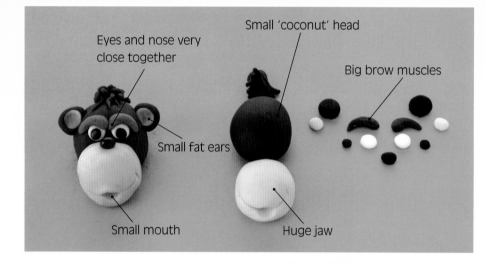

Eyes and nose very close together

Small 'coconut' head

Big brow muscles

Small fat ears

Small mouth

Huge jaw

Monkey

This cheeky money is almost the same as the mouse, but we make him with balls of different sizes. His tuft of hair at the top makes him look really cute. He can be made using eight balls and sausage shapes for the eyebrows.

Lion

The lion is, of course, the King of the jungle, but my lion has such a sweet innocent look, he couldn't harm anyone. He is made from six balls, plus one large and one small cone shape.

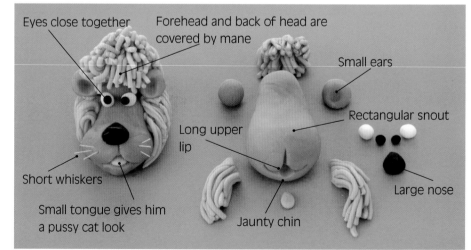

Eyes close together

Forehead and back of head are covered by mane

Small ears

Rectangular snout

Long upper lip

Large nose

Short whiskers

Small tongue gives him a pussy cat look

Jaunty chin

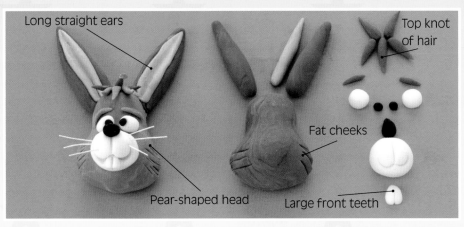

Long straight ears

Top knot of hair

Fat cheeks

Pear-shaped head

Large front teeth

Rabbit

This happy-go-lucky countryside resident is always ready for his next meal. He is full of character with his cross-eyed look and long ears. His eyes are close together and he has a distinctive goofy smile. He is made using eight cone shapes, five balls and four ovals.

Elephant

Every part of this huge animal is thick, fat and round. You could give him all sorts of expressions but this one is my favourite. The head is formed from a large cone, and then you pull out the trunk and continue to shape the face. The ears are made from oval shapes.

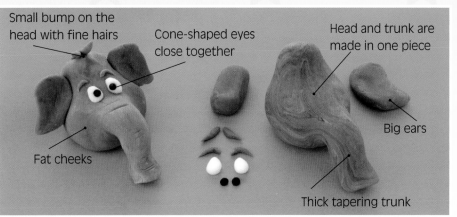

Small bump on the head with fine hairs

Cone-shaped eyes close together

Head and trunk are made in one piece

Big ears

Fat cheeks

Thick tapering trunk

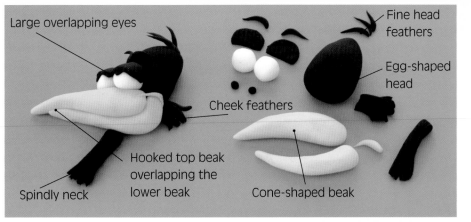

Large overlapping eyes

Fine head feathers

Egg-shaped head

Cheek feathers

Hooked top beak overlapping the lower beak

Cone-shaped beak

Spindly neck

Crow

What a classic cartoon character this bird is. The construction of the head is very simple, using three cone shapes, two circles and four balls, plus a few feathers.

Dog

I couldn't complete an animal book without including my favourite Old English sheepdog. He never fails to enchant, with a simple tussled head that makes him irresistible. He is made using a cone shape for the head, flattened at the front, and simply covered in a sunburst of tapered cone shapes.

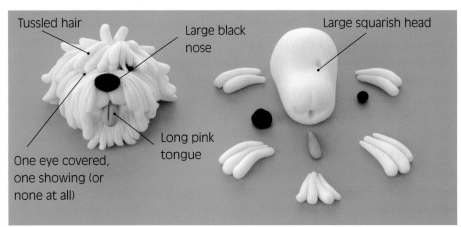

Tussled hair

Large black nose

Large squarish head

Long pink tongue

One eye covered, one showing (or none at all)

Cake Recipes

Before you can get on to the business of decorating your cake, first you need to bake it! While there are thousands of books on cake making for you to refer to, here are my tried-and-tested recipes for both sponge and fruit cakes and for the small cakes that you will find at the end of every project.

Madeira Cake

This is a very nice firm cake that will keep for up to two weeks, giving you plenty of time to decorate it. It can also be frozen. I use it because if you are placing sugarpaste characters on the top it stays firm and will not sink. The recipe here is for a plain cake, but you can flavour both the sponge and the buttercream (see page 24) to suit your own taste.

Tip

The temperatures stated and baking times given are for fan-assisted ovens, which is what I use. If you are using a conventional oven, you will need to adjust the timings accordingly.

Ingredients

For a 20cm (8in) round cake

* 115g (4oz) plain flour
* 225g (8oz) self-raising flour
* 225g (8oz) unsalted butter (at room temperature)
* 225g (8oz) caster sugar
* 4 eggs

Method

1 Pre-heat the oven to 160ºC (320ºF, Gas Mark 3). Grease the tin and line with greaseproof paper, then grease the paper as well.

2 Sift the flours into a large mixing bowl and add the butter and sugar. Beat together until the mixture is pale and smooth. Add the eggs and beat well, adding more flour if the mixture becomes too loose.

3 Spoon the mixture into the tin, and then make a dip in the top with the back of a spoon to prevent the cake from rising too much.

4 Bake in the centre of the oven for 1–1¼ hours. Test the cake (see tip opposite) and when it is cooked, remove it from the oven and leave it to stand in the tin for about 5 minutes, then turn it out on to a wire rack to cool fully.

5 Cover the cake around the sides and top with a coating of buttercream (see page 24), then cover with rolled sugarpaste (see page 26).

Rich Fruit Cake

This delicious cake improves with time, so always store it away before decorating it. I find it is generally at its best four weeks after baking, provided it is stored properly and fed with a little extra brandy!

Ingredients

For a 20cm (8in) cake

- ★ 575g (1lb 4¼oz) currants
- ★ 225g (8oz) sultanas
- ★ 85g (3oz) glacé cherries
- ★ 85g (3oz) mixed peel
- ★ 60ml (4tbsp) brandy
- ★ 285g (10oz) plain flour
- ★ 2.5ml (½tsp) salt
- ★ 1.25ml (¼tsp) nutmeg
- ★ 3.75ml (¾tsp) mixed spice
- ★ 285g (10oz) dark soft brown sugar
- ★ 285g (10oz) butter (at room temperature)
- ★ 5 eggs
- ★ 85g (3oz) chopped almonds
- ★ Grated zest of 1 orange and 1 lemon
- ★ 15ml (1tbsp) black treacle

Tip

Test whether a cake is ready by inserting a fine cake skewer into the centre. If the cake is ready, the skewer will come out clean, if not, replace the cake for a few more minutes and then test it again.

Method

1 Place all the fruit and peel into a bowl and mix in the brandy. Cover the bowl with a cloth and leave to soak for 24 hours.

2 Pre-heat the oven to 140°C (275°F, Gas Mark 1). Grease the tin and line with greaseproof paper, then grease the paper as well.

3 Sieve the flour, salt and spices into a mixing bowl. In a separate bowl, cream the butter and sugar together until the mixture is light and fluffy.

4 Beat the eggs and then add a little at a time to the creamed butter and sugar, beating well after each addition. If the mixture looks as if it is going to curdle, add a little flour.

5 When all the eggs have been added, fold in the flour and spices. Then stir in the soaked fruit and peel, the chopped almonds, treacle and the grated orange and lemon zest.

6 Spoon the mixture into the prepared tin and spread it out evenly with the back of a spoon.

7 Tie some cardboard or brown paper around the outside of the tin to prevent the cake from overcooking on the outside before the inside is done, then cover the top with a double thickness of greaseproof paper with a small hole in the centre to let any steam escape.

8 Bake the cake on the lower shelf of the oven for 4¼–4¾ hours. Do not look at the cake until at least 4 hours have passed, then test it (see tip above left).

9 When cooked, remove from the oven and allow to cool in the tin. When quite cold, remove from the tin but leave the greaseproof paper on as this helps to keep the cake moist. Turn the cake upside down and wrap in more greaseproof paper, then loosely in polythene and store in an airtight tin. Store in a cool, dry place.

10 You can feed the cake with brandy during the storage time. To do this, make a few holes in the surface of the cake with a fine skewer and sprinkle a few drops of brandy on to the surface. Reseal and store as above. Do not do this too often though or you will make the cake soggy.

11 Glaze the cake with apricot glaze (see page 25), then cover with rolled marzipan and sugarpaste (see pages 26–28).

Mini Cakes

These charming mini cakes are very popular and make the main cake go much further. Children love them, especially if they are made from sponge, which you can flavour to your personal taste. Ideally, use the Silverwood 5cm (2in) multi-mini pan set (see Suppliers, page 126), but if you don't have this you can just make one large cake and cut it into individual squares. Serve the cakes on 7.5cm (3in) cake cards.

Tip

There are special silicone liners available for the mini cake pans, but if you don't have them it is best to line the tins with greaseproof paper. Alternatively, grease the tins well, sprinkle them with flour, then shake off the surplus making sure all the greased surfaces are covered.

Ingredients

For 16 mini cakes or one 18cm (7in) cake to be cut into squares

★ 250g (9oz) self-raising flour
★ 250g (9oz) caster sugar
★ 250g (9oz) butter (at room temperature)
★ 4 eggs

Method

1 Pre-heat the oven to 180°C (350°F, Gas Mark 4), and prepare the cake pans (see tip above left).

2 Prepare the mixture as for the Madeira cake (see page 18) and half fill each cake pan. Bake in the centre of the oven for 15–20 minutes. You may wish to put a baking sheet on the bottom shelf to catch any drips. When cooked, remove from the oven and allow to cool to room temperature.

3 For perfect cubes, leave the cooled cakes in the pans and slice neatly across the tops with a long-bladed knife, using the pan tops as a cutting guide.

4 Remove the pans from the base and gently pull the halves apart to remove the cakes. You may need to run a thin-bladed knife around the top edges to release any slight overspill. Place the cakes on a wire rack. Once cooled, keep them covered, as they will dry out very quickly.

5 Cover each cake around the sides and top with a coating of buttercream (see page 24), then cover with rolled sugarpaste (see pages 26–27).

Cup Cakes

An alternative to the mini cakes is to use good old-fashioned cup cakes, which are simple to make and just as delicious. They can be iced rather than covered with buttercream and sugarpaste for a lighter, less indulgent treat.

Ingredients

For 12 cup cakes

* ★ 175g (6oz) unsalted butter
* ★ 175g (6oz) golden caster sugar
* ★ Finely grated zest of 1 orange
* ★ 2 large eggs
* ★ 100ml (7tbsp) milk
* ★ 175g (6oz) plain flour
* ★ 7.5ml (1½tsp) baking powder

Method

1 Pre-heat the oven to 180ºC (350ºF, Gas Mark 4).

2 Place all the ingredients into a food processor and cream together.

3 Arrange the paper cases inside two fairy cake tins and spoon the mixture into them, filling them two-thirds full.

4 Bake for 15 minutes until risen and springy to the touch, then remove from the oven and leave to cool.

5 Ice and decorate as desired.

Tip

The mini cakes can also be made in rich fruit cake. If you are making fruit versions it is best not to cut off the tops, so take care to fill the pans to the correct height. For fruit cakes, use apricot glaze and marzipan (see pages 25 and 28) instead of buttercream.

Other Recipes

Now you have your sugarpaste (see pages 8-9) and your cakes (see pages 18-21) ready and waiting, there are a few other recipes you will need in order to complete the projects in this book.

Pastillage

Pastillage is a form of sugarpaste that dries very hard, so is wonderful for building things like tables and chairs, houses and so on (see the baby carriage on page 84, for example). For the best results you have to give it 12 hours to dry on one side, and then turn it over for another 12 hours. You can colour it with paste food colour while it is still pliable, or spray colour on to it once it has dried. I have also painted it with liquid food colour to great success. As an alternative to using dry spaghetti to support your models (see page 14), you can make sugar sticks by rolling lengths of pastillage and cutting them up. You can buy pastillage powder from sugarcraft shops – just add water, following the instructions on the packet – but it is not difficult to make your own from this recipe.

Ingredients

To make 350g (12oz) of pastillage

★ 1 egg white (or the equivalent made up from dried egg albumen)
★ 280g (10oz) sifted icing (confectioners') sugar
★ 10ml (2tsp) gum tragacanth

Method

1 Place the egg white in a large mixing bowl and gradually add enough icing (confectioners') sugar to make a very stiff paste. Mix in the gum tragacanth and then turn the paste out on to the work surface and knead it into a smooth paste.

2 Store the pastillage in a polythene bag and then place it into a plastic airtight container. It can be kept in the fridge or frozen for up to a month.

For delicate models that need to stand up, it is best to use pastillage instead of regular sugarpaste, as it is stiffer and dries to a harder finish.

Tip

Dry pastillage pieces cannot be stuck together with edible glue (see opposite) alone. You need a much stronger paste, so mix together some edible glue and pastillage and work it into a creamy paste with a palette knife. Apply the strong glue to your pieces and leave them to dry completely.

Sugar Flower Paste

This is a good strong paste that can be rolled very thinly. It is ideal for making delicate objects such as facial details and flowers (see pages 49 and 111 for examples).

This hippo's glamorous long eyelashes are made from sugar flower paste, which can be rolled out much thinner than sugarpaste and dries hard so that they don't flop over.

Ingredients

* ✭ 25ml (5tsp) cold water
* ✭ 10ml (2tsp) powdered gelatin
* ✭ 500g (1lb 1½oz) icing (confectioners') sugar
* ✭ 10ml (2tsp) liquid glucose
* ✭ 15ml (1tbsp) gum tragacanth
* ✭ 10ml (2tsp) white vegetable fat (shortening)
* ✭ 1 egg white (or the equivalent made up from dried egg albumen)

Method

1 Mix the water and gelatin in a small heatproof bowl and leave to stand for 30 minutes. Then sift the icing (confectioners') sugar and gum tragacanth into the bowl of an electric mixer and fit the bowl to the machine.

2 Place the bowl with the gelatin mixture over a saucepan of hot water. Stir until all the ingredients have melted.

3 Add the dissolved gelatin mixture to the icing (confectioners') sugar with the egg white. Turn the machine on at its lowest speed. Beat until mixed and then increase the speed to maximum and continue beating until the paste is white and stringy.

4 Empty the paste out, then roll tightly in a polythene bag. Store it in an airtight container until required. It will keep for several weeks if stored correctly.

Edible Glue

This is the glue that holds sugarpaste pieces together, used in every project in this book. Always make sure your glue is edible before applying it to your cake.

Tip

Should you require stronger glue, use gum tragacanth as the base. Mix 5ml (1tsp) gum tragacanth powder with a few drops of water to make a thick paste. Store in an airtight container in the fridge.

Ingredients

* ✭ 1.25ml (¼tsp) CMC (Tylose) powder
* ✭ 30ml (2tbsp) boiled water, still warm
* ✭ A few drops of white vinegar

Method

1 Mix the CMC (Tylose) powder with the warm boiled water and leave it to stand until the powder has fully dissolved. The glue should be smooth and to a dropping consistency. If the glue thickens after a few days, add a few more drops of warm water.

2 To prevent contamination or mould, add a few drops of white vinegar.

3 Store the glue in an airtight container in the fridge and use within one week.

Buttercream

A generous coating of buttercream precedes the covering of sugarpaste on all sponge cakes. The classic version is flavoured with a few drops of vanilla essence, but you could substitute this for cocoa powder or grated lemon/orange zest to suit your particular taste.

Ingredients

To make 480g (1lb) of buttercream

★ 110g (4oz) butter

★ 30ml (2tbsp) milk

★ 350g (12oz) sifted icing (confectioners') sugar

Method

1 Place the butter into a mixing bowl and add the milk and any flavouring required.

2 Sift the icing (confectioners') sugar into a bowl a little at a time. Beat it after each addition until all the sugar has been incorporated. The buttercream should be light and creamy in texture.

3 Store in an airtight container for no more than one week.

Sweet and delicious, buttercream is simple to make and is the ideal covering for both large and mini sponge cakes before they are covered in sugarpaste.

Gum tragacanth, CMC (Tylose) powder, apricot glaze and confectioners' glaze are essential products that you will need to purchase before you begin sugarcrafting (see Suppliers, pages 126–7).

Essential Purchases

A visit to your local cake decorating or sugarcraft shop is a must – not only can you buy all the necessary products there, you will also come away very inspired! These products cannot be made at home with any great ease, and therefore need to be purchased.

✶ Gum tragacanth

This is a natural gum, which comes in the form of fine white powder used for thickening and strengthening sugarpaste for modelling (see page 9).

✶ CMC (Tylose) powder

Carboxymethylcellulose is a synthetic and less expensive substitute for gum tragacanth. It is used as a thickening agent when added to sugarpaste, and also used for edible glue.

✶ Apricot glaze

This glaze is painted on to fruit cakes before adding a layer of marzipan (see page 28). It is made from apricot jam, water and lemon juice, which is boiled then sieved. Although it would be possible to make your own, I don't know anyone who does, as it is so easy to use straight from the jar.

✶ Confectioners' glaze

This product is used to highlight the eyes, shoes, or anything you want to shine on your model. It is particularly useful if you want to photograph your cake, as it will really add sparkle. Apply a thin coat and let it dry, then apply a second and even a third to give a really deep shine. It is best kept in a small bottle with brush on the lid – this way the brush is submerged in the glaze and doesn't go hard. If you use your paintbrush to apply it, then you will have to clean it with special glaze cleaner.

Covering Cakes

Most beginners can successfully cover a cake with sugarpaste. However, a professional finish – a glossy surface free of cracks and air bubbles with smooth rounded corners – will only result from practise.

1 Prepare the cake with a layer of buttercream (see page 24) or apricot glaze and marzipan (see page 28) depending on whether it is a sponge or a fruit cake.

2 Take sufficient sugarpaste to cover the complete cake. The quantity required for each of the cakes in this book is given at the start of each project. Work the paste until it is quite soft and smooth, then place it on to a surface lightly dusted with icing (confectioners') sugar.

3 Roll out the paste with a non-stick rolling pin – spacing rods can be used to maintain a uniform thickness (**A**). The depth of the paste should be approximately 4mm (⅛in). As you roll the paste, move it regularly to ensure it has not stuck to the surface.

4 Measure the cake by taking a measuring tape up one side, over the top and down the other side. The sugarpaste should be rolled out in the shape of the cake to be covered (round for a round cake, square for a square cake and so on), and rolled out a little larger than the measurement just made.

Tip

When covering a cake, try to do it in natural daylight, as artificial light makes it more difficult to see flaws. Sometimes imperfections can be covered, but sometimes they will occur where you are not going to put decorations so you need to strive for a perfect finish every time. However, if things don't go to plan, don't worry; the sugarpaste can be removed and re-applied.

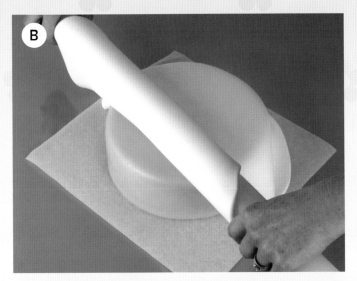

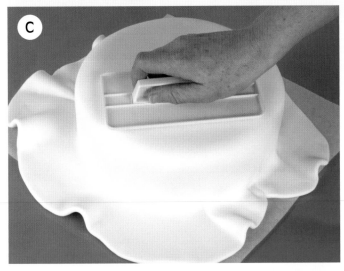

5 Lift and drape the paste over the cake using a rolling pin (**B**). Carefully lift the sides of the paste, brushing the top surface of the cake in one direction to eliminate any air trapped in between. Continue to smooth the top with the palm of your hand and then use a smoother (**C**).

6 For the sides, lift, flatten and rearrange any folds at the bottom removing any creases. Do not smooth downwards as this may cause a tear at the top edge. With your hand, ease the sugarpaste inwards at the base and smooth the sides with an inward motion using your hand and a smoother.

7 Trim the bottom edge with a marzipan knife. Trim the paste in stages as the icing shrinks back (**D**).

8 Check the surface and sides for any flaws and re-smooth if necessary. For air bubbles, insert a pin or fine needle into the bubble at an angle and gently rub the air out, then re-smooth to remove the tiny hole.

9 Once you are happy with the surface, use either the smoother or the palm of your hand and polish the top of the cake to create a glossy finish.

10 Ideally the sugarpaste should be left to dry for one or two days at room temperature before the cake is decorated.

Tip
Keep the dusting of icing (confectioners') sugar on the work surface very light; too much will dry out the paste and make it crack.

Covering the Cake Board

Moisten the board with cool boiled water, then roll out the specified quantity of sugarpaste to an even thickness, ideally using spacing rods (see page 12). Cover the board completely with sugarpaste using the same method as for the covering of the cake, smoothing the paste out and trimming the edges neatly with a marzipan knife. Some paste can then be saved by removing a circle from the centre of the board, which will be covered by the cake. For a professional finish edge the board with ribbon, securing with non-toxic glue.

Tip

An alternative method for covering a board involves placing the cake on to the board prior to covering them, then using a single piece of sugarpaste to cover them both. The sugarpaste needs to be rolled out much larger for this method.

Covering the cake board in sugarpaste gives your cakes a really professional appearance and allows you to add extra decorations and embellishments. As a finishing touch, edge the board with a length of ribbon.

Covering a Cake with Marzipan

A layer of marzipan is used on fruit cakes only. Sponge cakes should be covered with buttercream (see page 24) prior to covering with sugarpaste. For fruit cakes, coat first with apricot glaze (see page 25) as this will help the marzipan to stick. The quantity of marzipan required will depend on the size of the cake, but as a general guide, half the weight of the cake will give you the correct weight of marzipan.

1 Place the glazed cake on to a sheet of greaseproof paper. Place the marzipan in between spacing rods and roll to an even thickness large enough to cover the cake.

2 Lift the marzipan on to the rolling pin and place it over the cake. Push the marzipan into the sides of the cake using a cupped hand to ensure there are no air pockets.

3 Trim off any excess marzipan with a knife and then run cake smoothers along the sides and the top of the cake until they are straight.

4 Leave the marzipan to dry for one or two days in a cool temperature.

5 Before applying the sugarpaste, sterilize the surface of the cake by brushing the marzipan with a clear spirit such as gin, vodka or kirsch. Ensure the entire surface is moist; if there are any dry areas the paste will not stick to the marzipan and could result in air bubbles.

Tip

If you are using marzipan, make sure nobody eating the cake is allergic to nuts. This is very important as nut allergies are serious and can have fatal consequences.

Dowelling Cakes

A stacked cake is dowelled to avoid the possibility of the upper tiers sinking into the lower tiers. Several projects in this book require dowelling, including Purrfect Wedding (page 56), Baby Bear's Christening (page 80) and Mother's Day Surprise (page 104).

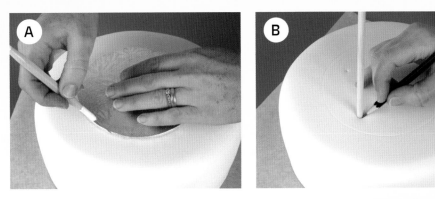

1 Place a cake board the same size as the tier above in the centre of the bottom tier cake. Scribe around the edge of the board (**A**) leaving an outline and then remove the board.

2 Using a wooden dowel, insert it vertically 2.5cm (1in) from the outline, down through the cake to the cake board below. Take a pencil and mark the dowel level with the surface of the cake (**B**) and then remove the dowel.

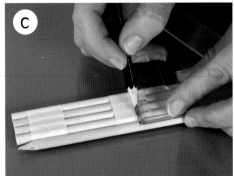

3 Tape together the number of dowels required (four is usually sufficient), and then draw a line across using the marked dowel as a guide (**C**). You can then saw across all the dowels to make them exactly the same length. Alternatively, you can unwrap the marked dowels and cut each of them separately with a pair of pliers or strong kitchen scissors.

4 Place the cut dowel back into the hole, then arrange the other dowels into the three, six and nine o'clock positions to the first one (**D**). Ensure that all the inserted dowels are level and have flat tops.

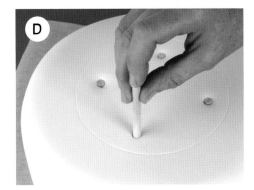

5 The cake board of the upper tier should rest on the dowels and not on the cake. The very slight gap in between the cake and the board of the upper tier will not be noticed and is normally covered by decoration.

Have Your Cake and Eat It!

You may well have cooked up a storm and made the perfect party cake, but how do you get your creation from kitchen to guest without a hitch? Storing the cake ahead of the event is the first consideration, then, if the party is not at your home, transporting it to the venue in one piece is of primary importance. Finally, some top tips follow on cutting the cake and removing items before eating it.

Cake Boxes

The most essential item for safe storage and transportation of your cake is a strong box designed for the job. You can buy special boxes for stacked cakes (see Suppliers, page 126) that open up at the front to enable the cake to slide inside. The front then closes and finally the lid is placed on the top. Make sure the box is deep and high enough to take the cake without damaging it when the lid goes on. To make the cake even safer inside the box, you can buy non-slip matting from most DIY stores. A piece of this cut to size and placed under the cake board will prevent it from moving around inside the box.

Tip

Keep your cakes away from direct sunlight at all times, as bright light will fade the sugarpaste.

Room Temperature

The temperature of the room the cake is stored in is crucial to its condition. If your house or the party venue is very humid it can be disastrous. You would do well to invest in a portable dehumidifier to keep the moisture at bay, especially during wet weather. Never think that your figures will benefit from leaving a heater on in the room; you will find that they become too warm and soft and will flop over.

Transportation

If you are transporting a cake, you need to be sure that the boot (trunk) of the car is high enough when closed, and the cake itself is made secure for the journey on a flat surface. Never put the cake on the back seat of the car, as this is not a level surface and the cake could be ruined when you apply the brakes. Remember too that if the vehicle gets too hot, it will affect the cake. It can melt buttercream and make sugarpaste soft.

Cutting the Cake

Many people have no idea how to begin to cut a cake, particularly a stacked one. If it is not cut properly it could end up in a pile of crumbs. The number of portions you require will have some bearing on the way you cut the cake. A simple way is to mark points on the edge of the cake at the desired intervals. Use a sharp serrated knife to cut across the cake and then downwards keeping the blade of the knife clean at all times. Then cut the section into smaller pieces.

The Decorations

If you wish to keep the decorations or figures on the cake, remove them before cutting. If they are to be stored, then do not put them into a plastic container, as they will sweat. Place them inside a clean cardboard box wrapped in tissue paper. Your decorations and figures will keep for a long time if you make sure they are kept in a dry atmosphere. Should you wish to display them, the best place is inside a glass-fronted cabinet where they will be safe.

Any decorations with wires attached should never be inserted directly into the cake as the metal can cause contamination. Instead, insert a cake pick, pushing it right into the cake until the top is level with the surface, then place the wires inside. Alternatively, you can make a mound of sugarpaste to insert wires into, and this can be hidden with more decoration.

When making figures for your cake, never insert cocktail sticks, always use dry raw spaghetti or make some sugar sticks from pastillage (see page 22). Remove any of these items before eating the figures. Children will always want to eat the figures, no matter how long it has taken you to make them.

Tip
If you wish to add candles to decorate your cake, always insert the candle holder into the cake first. When the candles are lit, they will prevent any wax from spilling on to the cake. Remove them before cutting the cake.

FAQ

Q: What if the road I am taking to deliver the cake is very bumpy?
A: Place the cake on a flat surface in the car. If necessary place a foam mat under the box and drive slowly!

Q: Is the footwell of the car the best place to transport a cake?
A: It is a good place, but make sure that there is nothing on the seat to slide off on to the cake – with disastrous consequences.

Q: What if it is a really hot day when the cake is delivered?
A: Keep the air conditioning on if you have it.

Q: If the cake is too heavy for me to lift at my destination what should I do?
A: Never try to lift a large cake on your own; ask if there is a truck available, or even a small table on wheels to place it on.

Q: Where is the cake best displayed?
A: Try to display the cake in a tidy, uncluttered area that will not detract from the cake.

Q: What should I look for once the cake has been assembled?
A: Check that the ribbon around the board is still lined up correctly and has not become loose or dislodged. Make sure your cake topper is securely fixed and perfectly upright.

Q: What shall I do if I make a mark on the cake while I am transporting it to its destination?
A: Always carry a fixing kit with you, which should include edible glue, a little royal icing in a bag, and a few spare decorations you can apply to cover the mark, depending on the design of the cake.

The Projects

Easter Bunnies
page 34

In the Spa
page 46

Purrfect Wedding
page 56

Good Luck
page 70

Easter Bunnies

The news is spreading, the Easter eggs have arrived and the rabbits are running as fast as they can to join in the feast before it is too late! This fun Easter cake is simple to make and the children will really enjoy helping you – particularly when it comes to making the grass, which is squeezed through a press to give this wonderful effect.

"I love chocolate Easter eggs - yummy!"

You will need

Sugarpaste

* ★ 1kg 50g (2lb 5oz) yellow
* ★ 450g (1lb) green
* ★ 310g (11oz) mid-brown
* ★ 60g (2oz) white
* ★ 50g (1¾oz) baby blue
* ★ 40g (1½oz) orange
* ★ 35g (1¼oz) brown
* ★ 15g (½oz) pink
* ★ 1g (⅛oz) black

Materials

* ★ 20cm (8in) square cake
* ★ 20 mini chocolate eggs
* ★ White vegetable fat (shortening)
* ★ White paste food colour
* ★ Edible glue (see page 23)
* ★ Non-toxic glue

Equipment

* ★ 25cm (10in) square cake drum
* ★ 7cm (2¾in) cake cards
* ★ 5cm (2in) round or oval cutter
* ★ Pretty ribbon: 15mm (½in) wide x 125cm (48in) long
* ★ Basic tool kit (see pages 12–13)

Tip

When covering the board, always remember to moisten it with a little cool boiled water first to help the sugarpaste to stick.

Covering the board and cake . . . .

1 Roll out 400g (14oz) of green sugarpaste to an even 3mm (⅛in) thickness.

2 Cover the board in the usual way (see page 28) using a cake smoother to give a level surface. Trim the edges neatly with a marzipan knife and set aside to dry. Save any leftover sugarpaste to use for decoration later.

3 Cover the prepared cake with 1kg (2lb 3¼oz) of yellow sugarpaste, rolled out to an even 5mm (⅛in) thickness. Trim the edges neatly with a marzipan knife.

4 Attach the cake to the centre of the board using strong edible glue. Edge the board with the pretty ribbon, securing it with non-toxic glue.

The fence . . . .

1 Mix together 30g (1oz) of mid-brown with 30g (1oz) of brown sugarpaste for a marbled effect (see page 10).

2 Roll out and cut four strips measuring 1 x 5cm (⅜ x 2in) to make the fence posts, shaping the top edges into points (**A**).

3 Attach three strips evenly spaced to the back of the cake, and then add some shorter pieces horizontally in between (**A**).

4 Cut the fourth strip diagonally at the top and lean it against the last upright post (**A**).

Tip
Set aside any sugarpaste left over from making the fence to use for the rabbit on the fence (see page 39).

The border

1 Attach the eggs by applying some edible glue along the base of the cake. Place four eggs evenly spaced on three sides of the cake below where the running rabbits will be. Do not add eggs to the side you have attached the fence to.

2 Create the grass by mixing together 45g (1½oz) of yellow sugarpaste left over from covering the cake with 45g (1½oz) of green sugarpaste.

3 Use a sugar press (or garlic press) to extrude short strands of grass and lay it down on to the work surface.

4 Use tool No.4 to chop off a few strands at a time to form clumps of grass. Position in between and around the eggs.

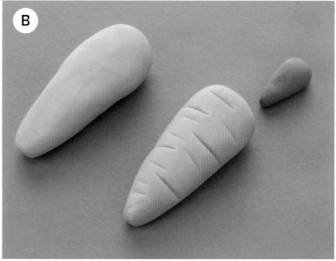

5 Make four large carrots using 32g (1oz) of orange sugarpaste. Take off 8g (¼oz) for each carrot, roll into a pointed cone shape and flatten at the top (**B**).

6 Using tool No.3, push into the top of each carrot to make a hole. Fill the hole with a small cone of green sugarpaste and flatten slightly with your finger. Mark the carrots with random lines using tool No.4 (**B**).

7 Secure the carrots to each corner of the board with edible glue. Make one smaller carrot in the same way and set aside.

Tip

Mix some white vegetable fat (shortening) into the paste to soften it before putting it into the press to make the grass. This will allow it to extrude easily without breaking the press.

The rabbit on the fence . . . .

1 For the body, take 10g (⅜oz) of the sugarpaste left over from making the fence and roll into a fat cone shape (**C**). Apply some edible glue and attach it to the edge of the cake above the fence.

2 For the back legs, equally divide 4g (⅛oz) and roll into small sausage shapes, narrowing around the ankle area to form a fat foot (**C**).

3 Push a short piece of dry spaghetti into the side of the rabbit's body and attach the legs, securing them to the fence.

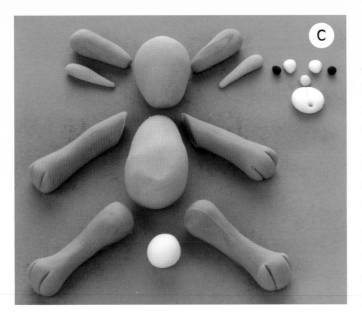

4 For the front legs, roll 2g (⅛oz) into a sausage shape. Make a diagonal cut in the centre to make two arms and secure these to the side of the rabbit and the edge of the cake. Using tool No.4, make two paw marks on each foot (**C**).

5 For the head, roll 6g (¼oz) into an oval shape. Mark a line down the centre front of the face, and add a small white muzzle and pink nose (**C**) at the top of the line.

6 For the eyes, roll two small white balls (**C**), and place them on the front of the face. Add two small black pupils (**C**) and press on lightly. Highlight the eyes with white paste food colour on the end of a cocktail stick or toothpick.

7 For the ears, roll two small cone shapes and flatten slightly with your finger. Roll two very thin cone shapes of pink sugarpaste (**C**) and place these on the top of the ears, pressing down gently.

8 Push a short piece of dry spaghetti into the end of each ear, and then push into the top of the head, securing with edible glue.

9 Push a piece of dry spaghetti into the top of the body, apply some edible glue and slip the head over the top.

10 For the tail, roll 1g (⅛oz) of white sugarpaste into a ball (**C**). Push a short piece of dry spaghetti into the back of the rabbit and then slip the ball over the top. Secure with edible glue.

The rabbit under the fence

1 For the body, roll 6g (¼oz) of mid-brown sugarpaste into a small cone and attach it under the fence.

2 For the tail, attach a small ball of white sugarpaste to the centre top of the body. Use tool No.4 to mark the back of the rabbit with a line.

3 For the back legs, equally divide 1g (⅛oz) of mid-brown sugarpaste and roll into two small cone shapes. Push the pointed ends into the sides of the rabbit.

The rabbit beside the fence

1 Take 8g (¼oz) of mid-brown sugarpaste and make the head, facial features, ears and just one paw, as described for the rabbit on the fence (see page 39).

2 Attach the small carrot (see page 38) to the board in front of this rabbit, securing with edible glue.

Tip

Take your time when placing the eyes, noses and mouths on your bunnies' faces – this is your chance to get their characters just right!

The running rabbits . . . .

1 **To help secure the completed running rabbits,** insert three short pieces of dry spaghetti in a line at regular intervals on three sides of the cake.

2 **To make the nine running rabbits** you will need 165g (5⅞oz) of mid-brown sugarpaste and 12g (½oz) of white sugarpaste. Allow 4g (⅛oz) of pink sugarpaste for the noses.

3 **For each body,** take off 6g (¼oz), roll into a small fat cone shape and place on to a small cake card (**D**). Push a short piece of dry spaghetti into the front to secure the head to at a later stage.

4 **To make the back leg,** roll 3g (⅛oz) into a sausage shape and narrow towards the foot. Using tool No.4, make the paw marks (**D**) and then attach to the back of the body.

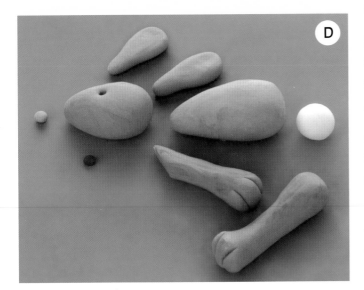

D

Tip

Give the rabbits a feeling of speed by positioning the legs in a running pose with the ears going backwards as if flapping in the wind.

5 **For the front leg,** roll 2g (⅛oz) into a sausage shape. Make a diagonal cut at one end and mark with tool No.4 as before (**D**). Attach to the front of the body, taking the foot over the back leg.

6 **For the head,** roll 5g (¼oz) into a small fat cone shape (**D**). Apply some edible glue and attach over the spaghetti at the front of the body.

7 **For the eye,** make a small hole with the end of your paintbrush (**D**) and drop a small ball of brown sugarpaste into it, securing with edible glue. Highlight the eyes with white paste food colour as before.

8 **For the nose,** add a small ball of pink sugarpaste (**D**) and then mark the whiskers with tool No.4. Add some edible glue to the back of the rabbit and slip it over the middle piece of spaghetti on the side of the cake. Press lightly against the cake and add more glue if required.

9 **For the ears,** take some of the remaining mid-brown sugarpaste and make two small cone shapes (**D**). Attach the first one to the side of the head and to the cake, then attach the outer ear.

10 **For the tail,** push a piece of dry spaghetti into the back of the rabbit and add a small ball of white sugarpaste (**D**).

Easter Bunnies 41

The sitting rabbit ·

1 To complete this rabbit you will need 50g (1¾oz) of mid-brown sugarpaste. Take off 25g (⅞oz) for the body and roll into a fat cone shape.

2 Push a length of dry spaghetti down through the centre, leaving 2cm (¾in) showing at the top. Push two small pieces of dry spaghetti into the side of the body at the top and bottom to secure the legs.

3 To make the back legs, equally divide 10g (⅜oz) of mid-brown sugarpaste and roll into a sausage shape. Narrow with your finger above the paw (**E**). Bend the shape and attach to the base of the body.

4 Turn up the right paw so that you can see the underside and then attach four small pink pads (**E**). Mark the left paw using tool No.4.

5 For the front legs, roll 6g (¼oz) into a sausage shape. Make a diagonal cut in the centre, keeping the ends nicely rounded for the paws. Attach the legs in a bent position over the spaghetti at the top of the body.

6 Take a mini egg and break off a piece using a knife to reveal the chocolate inside. Attach to the body and the paws with edible glue. Glue the bits of egg to the top of the cake.

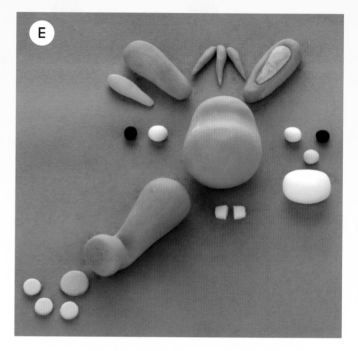

7 For the head, take off 6g (¼oz) and roll into an oval shape. Lightly indent the eye area with your finger keeping the cheeks fat (**E**), then push a short piece of dry spaghetti into the centre of the face. Roll 2g (⅛oz) of white sugarpaste into a ball (**E**), place it over the spaghetti and mark a small 'V' shape on the top.

8 Make the nose by rolling a small ball of pink sugarpaste (**E**) and gluing on the top of the muzzle.

9 To make the teeth, cut out two tiny squares of white sugarpaste (**E**), dip your brush into some edible glue and lift the teeth to the mouth area.

10 Make two ears and the eyes as described for the rabbit on the fence (see page 39). Turn the ears over at the top.

11 For the tail, add a small ball of white at the back.

12 For the hair, take 1g (⅛oz) of mid-brown sugarpaste and roll three small tapered cone shapes (**E**). Apply some edible glue in between the ears and attach the three cone shapes together.

The rabbit lying down

1 Make as for the sitting rabbit (see opposite) using 50g (1¾oz) of mid-brown sugarpaste but place the body in a horizontal position.

2 Break open an egg and attach it to the paw of the rabbit, then stick the pieces to the top of the cake using edible glue.

The blue basket

1 To complete the basket you will need 50g (1¾oz) of baby blue sugarpaste. Roll out the paste to a 0.5cm (⅛in) thickness. Cut out the base of the basket using a 5cm (2in) round or oval cutter. Place this on to a small cake card.

2 Using a piece of dry spaghetti, lightly mark 11 points evenly spaced around the base (**F**). Cut 11 lengths of dry spaghetti measuring 3cm (1¼in) long and push them into the points you have marked, keeping them upright and not too near the edge (**F**).

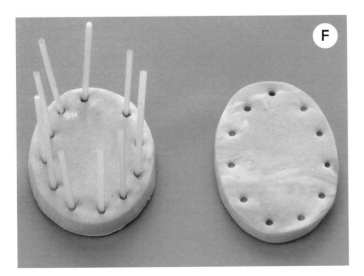

(**F**)

Tip

When creating a woven effect you must have an odd number of vertical posts to weave around; an even number will not work.

3 Roll a thin lace of the blue paste about 25cm (10in) long. Place one end of the lace inside the basket base, and then weave the remainder of the lace in and out of the spaghetti, always finishing with the end of the lace inside the basket (**G**).

4 Roll another lace the same thickness and place the point of this lace touching the end of the first lace, so that you begin and end at the same point. It doesn't matter how many laces you need, as long as you observe this rule.

5 Use the soft end of your paintbrush to press down the woven laces lightly, keeping them even. When you have reached the required height, level the spaghetti to the same height as the basket.

6 Twist together two thinner strips into a rope (**G**) and glue to the top of the basket to hide the spaghetti.

7 Fill the basket with eggs then make another twist for the handle (**G**). Attach with edible glue to the side of the basket.

8 Glue the basket into place on top of the cake and place the remaining eggs on top of the cake as shown.

9 Using 4g (⅛oz) of green sugarpaste, extrude more strands and add grass around the basket and the eggs.

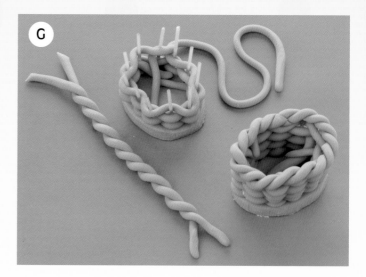

Tip
If there is a space between the eggs and the top of the handle, push a little foam underneath the handle to support it until it dries.

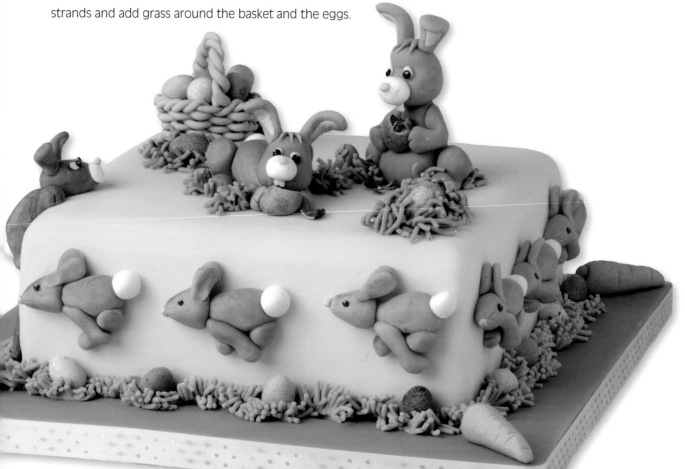

A Little More Fun!

Eastertide Treats

Bunny paw prints, mini carrots and the grass and eggs from the main cake can be used to decorate delicious little cup cakes too. You can try varying the colours of the icing, but make sure you keep to pretty spring pastels to match the fresh Easter theme.

In The Spa

Every girl deserves a bit of pampering once in a while and Miss Hippo is no exception. With her painted nails and fluttery eyelashes she is a sight to behold. This humorous cake will make a splash at any glamour girl's party, but be warned that the bubbles on the cake will need to be washed down with plenty of champagne bubbles!

"Ahhhh ... now this is the life, darling!"

You will need

Sugarpaste

★ 1kg 200g (2lb 10¼oz) white
★ 820g (1lb 13oz) red
★ 300g (10½oz) black
★ 60g (2oz) pale blue
★ 45g (1½oz) pink
★ 4g (⅛oz) yellow

Materials

★ 15cm (6in) round cake
★ Pink dust food colour
★ Metallic dust food colour in silver and gold
★ Magic Sparkle dust
★ Paste food colour in white, black and lime green
★ 1g (⅛oz) sugar flower paste (see page 23)
★ Confectioners' glaze
★ Edible glue (see page 23)
★ Non-toxic glue

Equipment

★ 30cm (12in) round cake drum
★ 25cm (10in) petal-shaped cake drum
★ PME ribbed rolling pin
★ 4cm (1½in), 3cm (1¼in), 2cm (¾in) and 1.5cm (½in) 1cm (⅜in) and 5mm (⅛in) round cutters
★ 1cm (⅜in) and 5mm (⅛in) blossom cutters
★ 1.5cm (½in) octagonal cutter (optional)
★ 1.5cm (½in) square cutter (optional)
★ Small heart cutter
★ Black ribbon 15mm (½in) wide x 2m (80in) long
★ Basic tool kit (see pages 12–13)

Covering the boards and cake

1 **To cover both boards** you will need 800g (1lb 12¼oz) of red sugarpaste. Take off 500g (1lb 1½oz) to cover the round board and proceed in the usual way (see page 28), trimming the edges neatly with a marzipan knife. Use the remainder to cover the petal-shaped board. Once the two boards are covered, set them aside and allow to dry.

2 Attach a length of black ribbon around the edge of each board, securing it with non-toxic glue. Secure the petal-shaped board to the centre of the round board with strong edible glue.

3 Before adding any covering to the cake, first take a sharp knife and hollow out the top of the cake making a gentle slope from the sides into the centre of the cake to a depth of 3cm (1¼in).

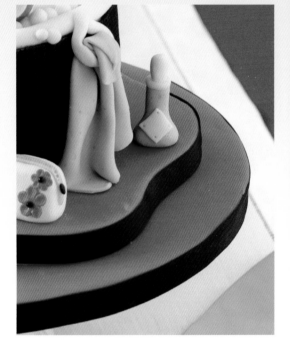

4 **Cover the cake** with 500g (1lb 1½oz) of white sugarpaste rolled out to an even thickness. Smooth it gently into the curve at the top, and then over the sides. Trim the base of the cake neatly.

5 **To cover the side of the cake**, take 250g (8¾oz) of black sugarpaste and roll it out into a strip measuring 7.5 x 55cm (3 x 21½in). Using a ribbed rolling pin, texture the surface. Apply some edible glue to the side of the cake and attach the strip, making a neat join at the back of the cake.

6 **Make a rolled edge** to fit around the top of the cake using 85g (3oz) of white sugarpaste rolled into a sausage shape. Apply some edible glue around the edge of the cake and secure the strip, making a neat join at the back. Place the cake on to a sheet of greaseproof paper until required.

The hippo

1 Mix together 220g (7¾oz) of white sugarpaste with 30g (1oz) of black to make a grey shade. Take off 225g (8oz) to make the hippo and set the rest aside to use for the decoration on the cosmetics later.

2 For the body, take off 85g (3oz) and roll into fat cone shape (**A**). Place this on top of the cake so that the head and shoulders are above the rim of the bathtub. Push a piece of dry spaghetti down through the body and into the cake, leaving 3cm (1¼in) showing at the top.

3 For the legs, take off a further 50g (1¾oz) of grey sugarpaste and roll into a sausage shape, making a straight cut in the centre. Flatten the rounded end with your finger (**A**). Bend the right leg at the knee and attach to the body. The foot will be hidden by the bubbles. Attach the left leg in a straight position showing the foot.

4 To make the arms, roll 35g (1¼oz) of grey sugarpaste into a fat sausage shape, and then make a diagonal cut in the centre. Flatten each rounded end with your finger (**A**). Push a short piece of dry spaghetti into the shoulder area of the hippo where the arms are to be attached.

5 Apply some edible glue and attach the left arm resting over the side of the tub. Bend the right arm at the elbow and attach to the shoulder. Rest the elbow on the side of the tub. Indent the hoof so that the bath brush will sit into it.

6 To make the pads for the left hand and left foot, roll out 10g (⅜oz) of pink sugarpaste. Cut out one 2cm (¾in) circle (**A**) and attach it to the end of the right foot. Then cut out a 1.5cm (½in) circle (**A**) and attach to the end of the left arm. Roll out 1g (⅛oz) of red sugarpaste into a thin lace and then cut out six fingernails each to a length of 5mm (⅛in) (**A**). Attach three to the left arm and leg.

7 For the head, take off 40g (1½oz) of the grey sugarpaste and roll into a cone shape (**A**). Slip the head over the spaghetti at the neck and secure with edible glue.

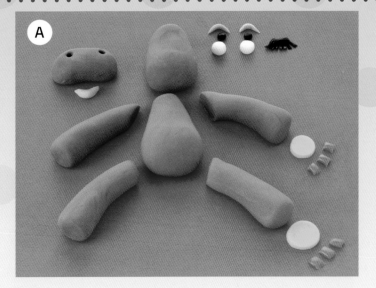

8 To make the cheeks, take off 15g (½oz) and roll into an oval shape. Gently squeeze the shape in the centre in between your finger and thumb to narrow it slightly (**A**). Push a short piece of dry spaghetti into the front of the head and attach the cheeks.

9 For the nose and mouth, push the end of your paintbrush into the top of the cheeks to make the nostrils and dust the cheeks with pink dust food colour. Make a very small banana shape in pink sugarpaste to form the bottom lip and attach under the cheeks (**A**).

10 For the eyes, roll two small balls of white sugarpaste (**A**) and glue them on to the face. Add two smaller balls of black sugarpaste for the pupils (**A**) and place them over the top, pressing gently to secure.

11 To make the eyelashes you will need 1g (⅛oz) of sugar flower paste coloured with black paste food colour. Roll the paste out thinly and cut into a strip measuring 2 x 1cm (¾ x ⅜in). Cut the strip in half and using a clean and sharp knife, cut into fine strips to form the eyelashes (**A**). Curl each eyelash over a paintbrush handle, or dowel until they have dried, and then glue them over the eye.

12 To form the eyelids, make two small banana shapes in grey sugarpaste, and then place over the eyelashes to secure. Highlight the eyes using some white paste food colour on the end of a cocktail stick or toothpick.

The turban and the bubbles

1 For the turban, roll out 18g (¾oz) of white sugarpaste and 5g (¼oz) of red sugarpaste. Cut out small circles from the red sugarpaste using 5mm (⅛in) and 1cm (⅜in) round cutters. Glue the circles on to the white sugarpaste in a random design. When you have finished, gently roll over the surface with your rolling pin to flatten.

2 Cut out a 4cm (1½in) circle from the decorated piece of sugarpaste (**B**) and attach this on top of the hippo's head. Using the remainder, cut out a piece measuring 15 x 3cm (6 x 1¼in). From the centre, taper the ends to a point and make a gentle fold in the centre (**B**).

3 Apply some edible glue to the head and wrap the turban around, bringing the ends to the front. Trim to a neat join.

4 For the ties, cut out two shapes using a 2cm (¾in) leaf cutter. Attach these to the front of the turban and add a small round ball in the centre (**B**).

5 To make the bubbles, first apply a thin coat of edible glue inside the bathtub, then roll 130g (4½oz) of white sugarpaste into small balls to fill the tub. Add some small bubbles to the hippo and the side of the tub. Dust the bubbles with Magic Sparkle dust.

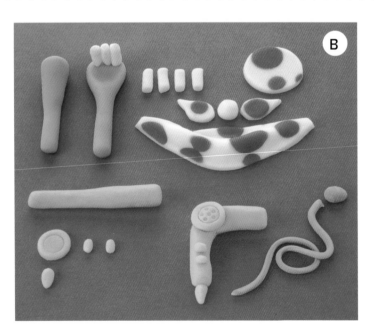

The bath brush

1 Colour 6g (¼oz) of white sugarpaste with lime green paste food colour and roll into a long cone. Flatten the widest end with your finger, making it into a wooden spoon shape (**B**). Gently twist a length of dry spaghetti through the handle and up to the end of the brush, leaving 1cm (⅜in) showing at the end of the handle.

2 To make the bristles, roll out 3g (⅛oz) of white sugarpaste into a thin lace, then cut off short lengths (**B**). Apply some edible glue to the brush and attach the bristles close together.

3 Secure the brush in an upright position in the hippo's right hand. Apply some edible glue to the centre of the petal-shaped board and place the cake in the centre.

The hairdryer

1 To complete the hairdryer you will need 15g (½oz) of pink sugarpaste. Take off 9g (⅜oz) and roll into a cone shape. Bend the cone into the shape of the dryer (**B**).

2 Cut out a 2cm (¾in) circle and place on the bend of the dryer. Take a 1.5cm (½in) round cutter and press this lightly into the centre of the circle. Make some dots in the centre using a piece of dry spaghetti. Add two small oval shapes on the handle for the switches (**B**).

3 Make a small cone shape and attach to the end of the handle (**B**). Secure the hairdryer to the board, resting on the side of the cake for support.

4 For the lead, roll a length of the pink sugarpaste into a thin lace and attach to the end of the handle (**B**). Curl the lead around and drape over the side of the board. Roll a small oval shape in pink for the plug and attach to the end of the lead (**B**).

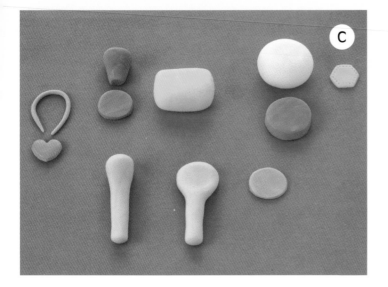

The pink bottle

1 Roll 17g (½oz) of pink sugarpaste into a ball, then using your fingers shape the ball into a rectangle shape measuring 3.5 x 2cm (1⅜ x ¾in). Make a straight cut at the top using a sharp knife (**C**).

2 For the stopper, roll 6g (¼oz) of grey sugarpaste into a fat cone shape and flatten the top with your finger (**C**). Using 2g (⅛oz) of grey sugarpaste, cut out a 2cm (¾in) circle (**C**). Place the circle on the top of the bottle and add the stopper, securing with edible glue.

3 For the tag, roll a very thin lace of grey sugarpaste, long enough to go around the neck of the bottle, bringing the two ends to the front. Cut out a small heart using 3g (⅛oz) of red sugarpaste and attach to the end of the lace (**C**).

4 Dust the stopper with silver metallic dust food colour. Place the completed bottle in front of the hairdryer on the board, securing with edible glue.

The cold cream

1 Roll 30g (1oz) of white sugarpaste into a ball and slightly flatten with your hand. Roll out 8g (¼oz) of grey sugarpaste and cut out a 3cm (1¼in) circle for the lid (**C**). Attach the lid to the top of the pot and dust with silver metallic dust food colour.

2 To make the label, roll out 2g (⅛oz) of pink sugarpaste and cut out an octagon, using a 1.5cm (½in) octagonal cutter or by hand (**C**). Attach the label to the jar with edible glue and add some stitch marks around the edges using tool No.12.

3 Place the completed cold cream jar on to the cake board, securing with edible glue. Roll some small bubbles in white sugarpaste, dust with Magic Sparkle dust and scatter on top of the lid and falling on to the board.

The hand mirror and the lipstick

1 For the hand mirror, roll 9g (⅜oz) of pale blue sugarpaste into a cone shape. Flatten the widest end with your finger (**C**). Roll out 2g (⅛oz) of grey sugarpaste and cut out a 2cm (¾in) circle for the mirror (**C**). Attach it with edible glue, then dust the top of the mirror with silver metallic dust food colour and secure to the board.

2 Make the base of the lipstick using 14g (½oz) of black sugarpaste. Roll into a thick sausage shape and then make it into a square shape with your fingers (**D**). It should measure 3 x 1.5cm (1¼ x ½in).

3 Roll out 4g (⅛oz) of yellow sugarpaste and cut out a square measuring 1.5cm (½in) with the cutter or by hand (**D**). Place this on top of the black base.

4 Roll the remainder of the yellow sugarpaste into a short sausage (**D**) and attach on top of the square. Push a piece of dry spaghetti down through the centre, leaving 2cm (¾in) showing at the top.

5 Take 3g (⅛oz) of red sugarpaste and roll into a short sausage shape. Pinch the top lightly to shape with your finger (**D**), and then slip it over the spaghetti.

6 Secure the completed lipstick to the cake board. Paint the red part with confectioners' glaze to make it shine.

D

In The Spa

The cosmetics bag

1 **For the bag**, roll 20g (¾oz) of white sugarpaste into a ball, and then gently flatten the shape. Continue to mould into the shape of a bag (**E**).

2 **For the decoration**, roll out 3g (⅛oz) of red sugarpaste and cut out two 1cm (⅜in) blossom shapes and one 5mm (⅛in) blossom shape. Using the end of your paintbrush roll each petal to shape (**E**). Attach the flowers to the bag and add a small ball of black sugarpaste into the centre of each flower.

3 **To make the zip fastener**, roll out 2g (⅛oz) of white sugarpaste and cut a thin strip to go over the top of the bag. Dust the strip with gold metallic dust food colour (**E**). Using tool No.12, run a line of stitch marks down the centre of the zip. Attach to the top of the bag.

4 **Make a small zipper tag** using a tiny amount of black sugarpaste rolled into a cone shape (**E**). Attach to the end of the zipper with edible glue. Secure the completed bag to the cake board.

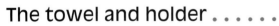

The towel and holder

1 **Make the towel** by rolling out 35g (1¼oz) of pale blue sugarpaste and cutting out a 9cm (3½in) square by hand. Place the square on the work surface in a diamond shape, and then push the handle of your paintbrush underneath to pleat it (**E**).

2 **For the holder**, roll 3g (⅛oz) of white sugarpaste into a short sausage shape. Bring the ends together (**E**) and secure with edible glue. Attach the holder to the side of the tub.

3 Gently push the end of the towel underneath the holder and fold over the top. Drape the end of the towel on to the board and secure with edible glue.

The blue lotion bottle

1 To make the blue bottle you will need 12g (½oz) of pale blue sugarpaste rolled into a fat cone shape. Flatten the cone with your fingers and shape the neck of the bottle (**F**). Push a piece of dry spaghetti down the centre of the bottle, leaving 1cm (⅜in) showing at the top.

2 For the stopper, take 2g (⅛oz) of white sugarpaste. Roll out and cut out a 1cm (⅜in) circle (**F**) and place this on top of the bottle over the spaghetti. Using the remaining white sugarpaste, roll into a small cone (**F**) and attach to the top of the circle. Position the bottle behind the towel on the cake board.

3 For the label, roll out 1g (⅛oz) of white sugarpaste and cut out a 1.5cm (½in) square (**F**). Glue to the front of the bottle and indent a dot into each corner using tool No.5.

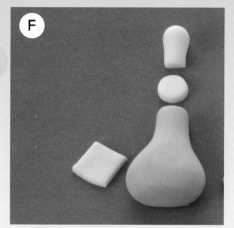

A Little More Fun!

Little Luxuries

These indulgent mini cakes are placed on their own little cake boards and are shaped and covered in much the same way as the large cake. The cosmetics bag, lipstick and pink bottle from the main cake become the focus here, but a scaled-down hippo's head could also be used. They are finished off with more sparkling bubbles. What better way to pamper all your guests?

Purrfect Wedding

What a sight these fabulous felines make!
The bride is a real diva with such a demure look and her
dapper groom is clearly devoted. Cat lovers will simply
adore this design, but you could easily substitute the cats
with other animals, or indeed humans, to make a truly
memorable wedding cake for any happy couple.

"The purrfect end to our purrfect day!"

You will need

Sugarpaste

★ 3kg 200g (7lb ¾oz) white
★ 400g (14oz) pink
★ 250g (8¾oz) black
★ 2g (⅛oz) blue

Materials

★ 10cm (4in), 20cm (8in) and
  25cm (10in) round cakes
★ Small and medium silver
  sugar dragees
★ Dust food colour in white
  sparkle, silver lustre and pink
★ Piping gel (optional)
★ Edible glue (see page 23)
★ Non-toxic glue

Equipment

★ 32cm (13in) round cake drum
★ 10cm (4in), 20cm (8in) and
  25cm (10in) cake cards
★ 5 cake dowels
★ 3cm (1¼in) oval cutter
★ 3cm (1¼in), 2.5cm (1in),
  13mm (½in) and 1cm (⅜in)
  round cutters
★ 5cm (2in) and 13mm (½in)
  square cutters
★ 2cm (¾in) and 13mm (½in)
  blossom cutters
★ Flower stamens
★ White ribbon 15mm (½in) wide
  x 115cm (45in) long
★ Narrow white ribbon 5mm
  (⅛in) wide x 15mm (½in) long
★ Basic tool kit (see pages 12–13)

Covering the board and cake

1 Roll out 500g (1lb 1½oz) of white sugarpaste to an even 3mm (⅛in) thickness. Cover the board in the usual way (see page 28) using a cake smoother to give a level surface and trim the edges neatly with a marzipan knife. Set aside to dry. Save any leftover sugarpaste to use for decoration.

2 Cover the prepared cakes with sugarpaste. To cover the 25cm (10in) cake, you will need 1kg (2lb 3¼oz) of white sugarpaste; 600g (1lb 5oz) for the 20cm (8in) cake and 300g (10½oz) for the 10cm (4in) cake.

3 Roll out the paste to an even 5mm (⅛in) thickness and cover each cake in the usual way (see pages 26–27). Attach the largest cake to the centre of the board using strong edible glue then follow the steps for dowelling a stacked cake on page 29. Edge the board with the white ribbon, securing with non-toxic glue.

Tip

White sugarpaste is not usually very bright, so if you would prefer a brighter white add some whitener, which is available from sugarcraft shops.

The buckles and collar borders

1 **For the buckles**, add 5g (¼oz) of black sugarpaste to 25g (⅞oz) of white and mix together into a grey shade. Roll out to 4mm (⅛in) in thickness. Cut out a square measuring 2.5cm (1in), and then take out the centre using a 13mm (½in) square cutter (**A**). Make three.

2 Apply some edible glue very thinly to the top of the buckle, and then place two rows of small sugar dragees around the buckle (**A**). Set aside to dry.

3 **To complete the three cat collars** you will need 350g (12¼oz) of pink sugarpaste. Take off 70g (2½oz) and roll a long sausage shape, and then roll out into a strip measuring 38 x 2.5cm (15 x 1in). Stitch mark along both edges using tool No.12 and then cut one end into a curve (**A**).

4 **Attach the collar to the smallest cake** using edible glue and overlap the ends. Attach the buckle carefully with edible glue. Using the end of your paintbrush indent evenly spaced holes all around the collar. Apply a little edible glue inside each hole and push a medium sugar dragee inside (**A**).

5 **For the next collar**, take off 125g (4½oz) of pink sugarpaste and then roll out a strip measuring 70 x 2.5cm (27½ x 1in). Complete as for the first collar, positioning the buckle to the right of the first one.

6 **For the largest collar**, roll out 150g (5¼oz) of pink sugarpaste into a strip measuring 87 x 2.5cm (34¼ x 1in). Complete as for the other two collars, positioning the buckle to the right of the last one.

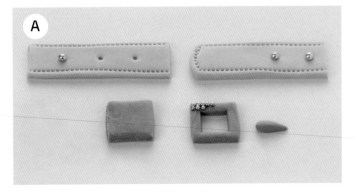

A

Tip

Do not get any glue on the top of the dragees otherwise the silver will disappear. Try lifting them with a clean brush dipped into cool boiled water, keeping the brush barely moist.

The paw prints

1 Cut out 16 pads using 125g (4½oz) of white sugarpaste and a 3cm (1¼in) oval cutter. Push the 1cm (⅜in) round cutter into the lower edge to shape the pad.

2 For the toes, cut out four small circles using the 1cm (⅜in) round cutter. Arrange a row evenly spaced around the top of the largest cake, and then place a row at the bottom so that they are in between the top row. Secure the parts with edible glue, and then dust carefully with white sparkle dust food colour using a dry brush.

The bride

1 To complete the bride's body you will need 240g (8½oz) of white sugarpaste mixed with 10g (⅜oz) of black sugarpaste to make a pale grey shade.

2 For the body, take off 70g (2½oz) and roll into a smooth ball. When it is completely smooth, roll it into a fat cone shape (**B**). Place the cone in the centre of the small cake and push a piece of dry spaghetti through the centre, leaving 2cm (¾in) showing at the top.

3 Push a short piece of dry spaghetti into the hip area ready to attach the legs. Using the end of your paintbrush, make a navel.

4 To make the legs, roll 60g (2oz) into a sausage shape, making a diagonal cut in the centre, and a straight cut at each end (**B**). Attach the left leg at the hip, and then push a piece of dry spaghetti through the lower half of the leg to keep it straight.

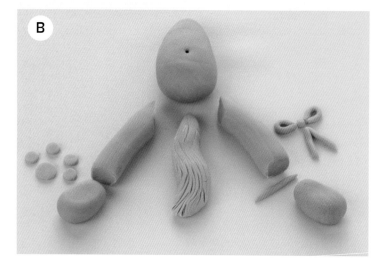

B

5 Make the paw by rolling 6g (¼oz) into a fat cone shape (**B**). Mark the toes using tool No.4 and add some pads by rolling some small pinks balls and then flattening them (**B**). Apply some edible glue to the base of the leg, and then slip the paw firmly over the spaghetti.

6 Roll a thin lace of pink and glue around the join. Make a small tie and two loops to form the bow, adding a ball in the centre to finish (**B**). Bend the right leg at the knee area and cross it over the left. Complete to match the left leg. Set the rest of the grey sugarpaste aside.

The bride's skirt and tail

1 For the skirt, take 110g (3⅞oz) of white sugarpaste and roll into a ball, and then into a sausage shape. Using a rolling pin, roll the sugarpaste into a slightly curved shape until it measures 30 x 9cm (12 x 3½in) (**C**).

2 Apply some edible glue around the waist area and the top of the legs. Trim the ends straight and turn them under at both ends (**C**). Loosely gather the top to fit all around the bride's body.

3 Tuck the skirt under to rest on top of the legs, keeping the folds soft and flowing (**C**). The side of the skirt should fall to the side of the bride. Leave the navel showing.

4 For the tail, roll 20g (¾oz) of grey sugarpaste into a fat cone shape. Using the curved end of tool No.4, mark the tail to look like fur (**B**). Attach the tail to the back of the bride, allowing it to fall over the side of the cake.

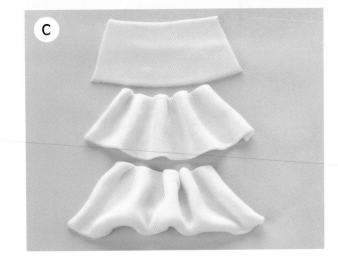

Tip

Use the soft brush end of your paintbrush to arrange the folds of the dress, as it will not mark the sugarpaste.

The bride's bodice and arms

1 For the bodice, roll out 40g (1½oz) of white sugarpaste and cut out two 5cm (2in) squares. Using a textured rolling pin, roll over the top of each square (**D**). Take one square and attach it to the back of the bride. Using tool No.4, mark a straight line down the seam on either side and remove the excess sugarpaste.

2 Place the second square on to the work surface and mark a fine line down the centre. Cut out a 'V' shape at the top and a smaller inverted 'V' at the bottom. Make a diagonal cut on each side at the shoulder. This should now be a butterfly shape (**D**).

3 Attach the front of the bodice to the bride with edible glue, and trim the sides if they overlap, removing the excess sugarpaste. The seams should join together neatly. The opening at the front of the bodice should show the navel, and the points rest over the skirt. Add four small silver dragees (**D**) for buttons on the front.

4 For the sleeves, roll out 8g (¼oz) of white sugarpaste into a sausage shape measuring 4cm (1½in). Cut in half and set aside. Roll out a further 12g (½oz) and roll over with the textured rolling pin. Cut out two circles using a 2.5cm (1in) round cutter. Make a straight edge on each circle and glue to the sleeve shape (**D**).

5 Push a short piece of dry spaghetti into the body at the shoulder and apply some edible glue. Slip the sleeves over to secure. Push another piece of dry spaghetti into the end of each sleeve to take the arms.

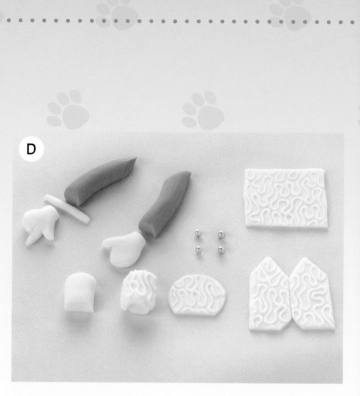

D

6 Make two arms using 30g (1oz) of the grey sugarpaste equally divided. Roll into a sausage shape and make a straight cut in the centre and at each end (**D**). Push the left arm over the spaghetti at the base of the sleeve. Bend the right arm at the elbow. Slip the top of the arm over the spaghetti at the base of the sleeve, and then push a length of dry spaghetti through the lower arm and into the skirt, leaving 1cm (⅜in) showing at the top to take the glove.

7 To make the gloves, take 12g (½oz) of white sugarpaste and divide equally. Roll into a cone shape and flatten the end with your finger. Take tool No.4 and cut out a 'V' shape for the thumb (**D**). Cut out one finger, and gently roll it to remove the square edges. Mark the other three fingers with tool No.4.

8 Apply some edible glue to the end of the arms and slip the gloves over the spaghetti. The right glove will rest on the top of the cake; the left one should have the hand slightly open to hold the flowers. Make a thin lace to go over the seams in-between the glove and the arm (**D**).

The bouquet

1 Roll out 7g (¼oz) of white sugarpaste and then cut out a 5cm (2in) square. Fold the square into a cone shape, just like an icing bag. Taper the bottom but keep the top open (**E**). Drop a small ball of sugarpaste into the cone to fill it up.

2 To make the flowers you will need 7g (¼oz) of pink sugarpaste and a 13mm (½in) blossom cutter. Cut out several flowers and, using the end of your paintbrush, roll each petal to widen it. Add a small ball of white sugarpaste in the centre (**E**). Make six flowers.

3 Apply some edible glue to the top of the cone and add the flowers to the top. Apply some edible glue and secure the bouquet to the hand of the bride.

The bride's head and headdress

1 To make the head, roll 35g (1¼oz) of grey sugarpaste into a smooth ball. Indent the eye area and pinch the cheeks out with your fingers (**E**). Push a piece of dry spaghetti into the centre of the face. Add a 3g (⅛oz) white ball and press it on to the spaghetti.

2 To create the mouth, mark the centre of the white ball with a line and, using tool No.11, mark a smile on either side of the line at the bottom to form the mouth (**E**). Using pink sugarpaste, roll two tiny teardrop shapes for the top lip, placing the fattest ends together in the centre, and then make a small banana shape for the bottom lip (**E**). Secure to the mouth with edible glue.

3 Make the nose by rolling a small ball of pink sugarpaste (**E**) and glue to the face at the top of the line.

4 For the eyes, roll two white balls and then make them into teardrop shapes (**E**). Place them just above and on either side of the nose. Add two small balls of blue sugarpaste for the pupils (**E**). Add eyelids to half cover the eyes using small cone shapes of the grey sugarpaste (**E**). Make two curved banana shapes for the eyebrows and attach above the eyes (**E**).

5 To make the ears, roll two small cone shapes, and then add a tiny pink cone shape inside (**E**). Make a straight cut at the base of the ear. Push a piece of dry spaghetti into the side of the bride's head, apply some edible glue and slip the ears over the spaghetti.

6 For the hair and whiskers, add four thin tapered cone shapes on the top of the head for the hair (**E**).Take six flower stamens and cut off the tops. Push three into each side of the face to make the whiskers.

7 For the headdress, roll out 3g (⅛oz) of white sugarpaste and cut out a flower shape using a 2cm (¾in) blossom cutter (**E**). Then cut out a pink shape using the same cutter. Then add a small pink flower shape in the centre using the 13mm (½in) blossom cutter (**E**).

8 Using the end of your paintbrush, thin out the edges of the petals and then attach the small flower inside the large one, adding a dot of white at the centre (**E**). Dust the petals with pink dust food colour and a clean brush. Attach the flower to the top of the bride's head.

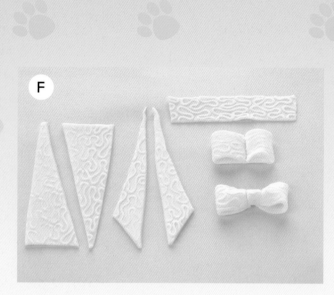

F

9 To make the train, roll out 20g (¾oz) white sugarpaste into a rectangle shape. Texture the surface with the rolling pin. Cut out two strips measuring 12 x 4cm (4¾ x 1½in). Make a diagonal cut from the bottom right-hand corner to the top left-hand corner. Place the narrow ends together and make diagonal cuts at the widest ends (**F**).

10 Attach the train to the top of the bride's head, resting the ends on top of the cake on either side of the tail.

11 For the bow, roll out 10g (⅜oz) of white sugarpaste into an oblong shape. Texture the surface of the paste to match the train. Cut a strip measuring 9 x 2cm (3½ x ¾in). Turn the strip over to the wrong side, apply edible glue to the centre and fold the ends into the centre (**F**). Turn over to the right side and pinch the centre of the bow to narrow it. Mark the bow using tool No.4. Attach to the bride's head over the top of the train.

The champagne glass

1 Take 3g (⅛oz) of white sugarpaste and roll into a long cone shape. Push tool No.3 inside the thickest end and hollow out to shape the top of the glass (**H**).

2 Take a piece of dry spaghetti and pass it through the stem up into the glass to support it (**H**). Break off any spaghetti showing at the top, and leave a very short piece showing at the bottom. Cut out a small round shape for the foot of the glass and attach to the stem (**H**). Set aside to dry.

The groom

1 To complete the groom you will need 225g (8oz) of black sugarpaste, and 115g (4oz) of white sugarpaste. Roll 45g (1½oz) of black sugarpaste into a cone shape for the body (**G**) and place this on top of the cake.

2 Push a length of dry spaghetti down through the centre of the body leaving 2cm (¾in) showing at the top. Push a short piece of dry spaghetti on either side of the lower body ready to support the legs.

3 For the legs, take off 60g (2oz) of black sugarpaste and roll into a sausage shape 20cm (8in) long. Make a diagonal cut in the centre and flatten the other end with your finger (**G**). Push a short piece of dry spaghetti into the leg.

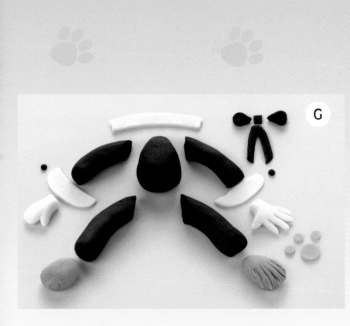

4 Attach the right leg first. Bend the left leg at the knee so that it will rest on top of the right one. Push a short piece of dry spaghetti into the side of the cake and then press the lower leg on to it to prevent the leg from slipping.

5 To make the feet, make up some grey sugarpaste by mixing together 80g (2⅞oz) of white sugarpaste with 15g (½oz) of black. Take off 24g (⅞oz), divide equally and roll into fat cone shapes. Set the rest aside for later.

6 Using the rounded end of tool No.4, mark each foot with lines to look like fur (**G**). Apply some edible glue to the top of the paw and slip over the spaghetti at the base of each leg. Using 2g (⅛oz) of pink sugarpaste, attach a ball for the pad and four small ones for the toes (**G**).

The groom's waistcoat and tailcoat

1 For the waistcoat, roll out 16g (½oz) of pink sugarpaste, and texture with the rolling pin. Cut out a square measuring 5cm (2in) and mark a faint line down the centre. Cut out an inverted 'V' shape at the bottom of the waistcoat (**H**). Attach the finished piece to the front of the groom's body.

2 For the tailcoat, take off 45g (1½oz) of black sugarpaste, roll out and cut to shape (**H**). The finished shape should measure 9 x 13cm (3½ x 5in). Before you attach it to the body, try it for size, as you do not want it to cover the front of the waistcoat. Apply edible glue to the body at the back and sides, placing the coat first at the back and then bring it to the front.

3 Make the groom's tail in the same way as the bride's tail (see page 61), securing it to the back of the tailcoat with edible glue.

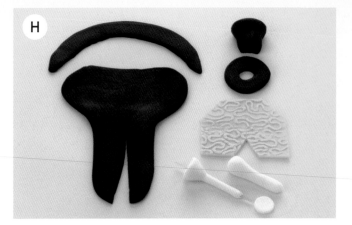

4 Make the collar to fit around the edge of the coat in a curved shape (**H**). Take 10g (⅜oz) of black sugarpaste and roll it into a thin tapered sausage shape, long enough to fit all around the edge of the coat. Roll it out flat and then re-shape it into a curve. Trim the edges with a cutting wheel, bringing it to a point at each end. Secure the collar with edible glue and hide any raw edges showing on the coat.

5 Make the buttonhole using the 13mm (½in) blossom cutter. Cut out a small white flower and soften the edges with your paintbrush. Place a small ball of pink in the centre and attach to the lapel with edible glue.

Tip

Because the groom is sitting so close to the bride, you may find it easier to model him on the edge of a small round dummy first, and then transfer him to the cake later.

The groom's arms

1 Take off 32g (1oz) of black sugarpaste and roll into a sausage shape measuring approximately 13cm (5in) long. Make a diagonal cut in the centre and a straight cut at each end (**G**).

2 Attach the left arm to the body in a bent position, resting on the left leg. Next, take the right arm and bend it so that the hand will be in an upright position.

3 Attach the right arm to the top of the body, and then push a long piece of dry spaghetti into the wrist area, pushing it down into the forearm and then into the body, so that it will stay upright. Leave a short piece of spaghetti showing at the wrist to support the hand.

4 For the hands you will need 10g (⅜oz) of white sugarpaste equally divided. Roll into a ball and then into a cone shape. Flatten the cone with your finger and cut out the thumb (**G**).

5 Divide the rest of the hand into four fingers, and then roll and lengthen them to remove the edges (**G**). Cut off at the wrist and slip over the spaghetti on the arm.

Tip

When cutting out clothes to fit your figures, make sure that the piece for the front (and back if required) is big enough to fit from the neck to the hip, and halfway around the body from one side seam to the other.

6 Make the shirt cuffs by equally dividing 2g (⅛oz) of white sugarpaste. Roll into a small sausage shape 2.5cm (1in) long and flatten with a rolling pin (**G**). Apply some glue around the wrists and attach the cuffs. This will hold the hands firmly to the arms. Add small black balls (**G**) on the outside edges for the cufflinks.

7 Place the champagne glass into the right hand, shaping the fingers around the stem of the glass. Support the whole arm with foam if necessary until dry. Fill the glass with some piping gel to look like liquid, or alternatively roll tiny balls of white sugarpaste to look like bubbles to fill the glass.

The groom's head, hat, collar and bow tie

1 To complete the head you will need 35g (1¼oz) of grey sugarpaste left over from earlier. Follow the directions as for the bride's head (see page 63), making the lips less full and feminine.

2 To make the hat, take off 13g (½oz) of black sugarpaste. Roll out and cut a circle using a 3cm (1¼in) round cutter. Take out the centre of the circle with a 13mm (½in) round cutter (**H**). Apply some edible glue to the groom's head and place the brim of the hat on the top. Make the crown using 6g (¼oz) of black sugarpaste rolled into an oval shape. Flatten the top with your fingers and widen it (**H**). Glue to the centre of the brim.

3 For the shirt collar, cut out a strip of white sugarpaste long enough to go around the neck and meet at the front under the groom's chin (**G**). Attach with glue and turn over the corners at the top.

4 For the bow tie, roll out 3g (⅛oz) of the black sugarpaste and cut out a strip 5mm (⅛in) wide. Make a tie and two loops (**G**). Attach under the collar and add a small square in the centre of the bow to finish.

The horseshoe

1 Roll out 8g (¼oz) of grey sugarpaste left over from making the groom and cut out a 2.5cm (1in) circle. Take out the centre of the circle with a 13mm (½in) round cutter.

2 Cut an opening at the top of the shape and then mark the nails with a piece of dry spaghetti (**I**), see overleaf). Dust with silver lustre dust food colour and set aside to dry.

The playful kitten

1 To complete the kitten you will need 55g (2oz) of white sugarpaste mixed with 5g (¼oz) of black sugarpaste to make a pale grey shade, and 3g (⅛oz) of pink sugarpaste.

2 Make the body by rolling a 22g (¾oz) ball of grey sugarpaste into a cone shape measuring 6cm (2⅜in) long. Place the cone shape down on to the work surface. Roll a thin cone shape using 3g (⅛oz) of white sugarpaste and glue to the top of the body (**I**).

3 To make the back legs, take off 12g (½oz) equally divided and roll into a cone shape. Keeping the end rounded, narrow at the ankle area by rolling the leg backwards and forwards with your finger (**I**). Push a short piece of dry spaghetti into the side of the kitten's body and attach the two back legs in an upward position. Add small pink pads and toes to each foot (**I**).

4 For the front legs, roll 6g (¼oz) of grey sugarpaste into a short sausage shape measuring 5cm (2in) long, marking the paws with tool No.4 (**I**). Make a diagonal cut in the centre and glue to the upper body into the required position. Add the pink pads and toes as before.

5 Add a tail to the back of the kitten using 4g (⅛oz) of grey sugarpaste rolled into a tapered cone shape. Mark the end of the tail to look like fur using tool No.4 (**I**).

6 For the head, roll a 10g (⅜oz) ball of grey sugarpaste (**I**). Push a short piece of dry spaghetti into the centre of the face and apply a little glue around it.

7 To make the front of the face, roll a 2g (⅛oz) ball of white sugarpaste and slip it over the spaghetti, pressing it on with your finger. Take tool No.4 and mark a line down the centre (**I**).

8 For the mouth, add a smile on either side of the line with tool No.11. Roll a tiny oval shape of white sugarpaste and flatten with your finger then glue to form the jaw (**I**). Push a piece of spaghetti into the mouth area to make a hole and add a tiny pink cone shape for the tongue.

9 For the eyes and nose, add two small balls of blue for the eyes, and one of pink for the nose (**I**). Make two small cone shapes for the ears, and add a thin cone shape of pink sugarpaste to the inside (**I**). Attach to the side of the kitten's head, securing with tool No.1, which will indent the ear into the correct shape. Push a short piece of dry spaghetti into the top of the body and slip the head over, securing with edible glue.

10 To make the collar, roll out a very small strip of pink sugarpaste (**I**) and glue to the front of the kitten. Add some small sugar dragees (**I**) to finish.

11 Take the length of narrow ribbon and wrap it around the kitten's legs. Bring the two ends of the ribbon to the side of the cake and attach with edible glue. Secure the horseshoe over the ends.

A Little More Fun!

Hearts' Delights

These charming mini cakes reflect the theme of the large cake beautifully, and will surely win the hearts of your guests. They can be made in fruit or sponge cake using the Silverwood multi-mini pan set (see Suppliers, page 126). Why not make one for each of the bridesmaids as a special thank you?

Good Luck

Making a cake to wish someone luck really shows that you care. The horseshoes and shamrocks on this colourful cake are certain to bring good fortune to anyone who takes a bite. The pony is enjoying her apples and the squirrel is the perfect country companion. The horse theme makes this ideal for a child's riding competition, but it would be equally good for exams, interviews or any occasion where luck is needed.

"I need a snack after all that horsing around."

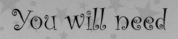

You will need

Sugarpaste

* 1kg (2lb 3¼oz) Lincoln green
* 225g (8oz) mid-brown
* 200g (7oz) brown
* 150g (5¼oz) white
* 80g (2⅞oz) red
* 65g (2¼oz) black
* 20g (¾oz) yellow
* 1g (⅛oz) orange

Materials

* 25 x 20cm (10 x 8in) oval cake
* Dust food colour in light brown, white and silver lustre
* Paste food colour in bright green, white and chestnut
* Liquid food colour (or food colour pens) in brown and yellow
* Confectioners' glaze
* White vegetable fat (shortening)
* Edible glue (see page 23)
* Non-toxic glue

Equipment

* 30 x 25cm (12 x 10in) oval cake drum
* 15cm (6in) cake cards
* 1cm (⅜in) and 8mm (¼in) blossom cutters
* 2.5cm (1in) and 1cm (⅜in) round cutters
* 1cm (⅜in) leaf cutter
* Small shamrock cutter (optional)
* Brown satin ribbon 15mm (½in) wide x 1m (40in) long
* Basic tool kit (see pages 12–13)

Covering the board and cake ....

1 To cover the board you will need 60g (2oz) of black sugarpaste, 60g (2oz) of mid-brown sugarpaste and 60g (2oz) of white sugarpaste. Mix together some white and black to make a grey marbled effect. Mix together some brown and black and then leave some of the sugarpaste a single colour. This will make the random pattern more interesting (**A**).

2 Apply some edible glue around the edge of the board, and then roll some balls of the grey and brown and black mixture, and some single coloured balls (**A**). Flatten the balls with your finger and secure them to the board in a random fashion making sure you leave no spaces between the shapes. Keep the design to 3cm (1¼in) wide.

3 When you have covered the area, roll over it lightly with your rolling pin, and then trim the edges with a marzipan knife, keeping it upright.

4 To cover the cake you will need 1kg (2lb 3¼oz) of Lincoln green sugarpaste. Roll out and cover the prepared cake in the usual way (see pages 26–27), taking care to trim the edges neatly. Secure the cake to the centre of the board with strong edible glue then dust the top of the cake with light brown dust food colour.

5 Attach the ribbon around the base of the cake and board, securing it with edible glue on the cake and non-toxic glue on the board.

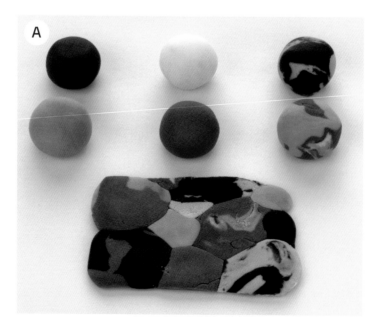

A

The apple border

1 Equally divide 75g (2½oz) of red sugarpaste into five portions. Roll each portion into a ball and then flatten into a domed shape with the palm of your hand. Push a hole into the top with the end of your paintbrush (**B**).

2 Using a soft brush and a mixture of brown and yellow liquid food colour, or food colour pens if you prefer, shade the top and base of the apple (**B**). Roll out 4g (⅛oz) of brown sugarpaste into a lace, and then cut five short stalks (**B**). Glue the stalks into the holes at the top of the apples.

3 Make a vibrant shade of green using 70g (2½oz) of white sugarpaste mixed with a bright green paste food colour. Roll out the paste and cut out five green leaves using a small leaf cutter, then set the remainder aside. Using tool No.4, vein the leaves, marking them down the centre and on either side of the line (**B**).

4 Push a short piece of dry spaghetti into the centre front of the cake. Apply some edible glue to the back of an apple and slip over the spaghetti. Space out two more pieces of dry spaghetti 10cm (4in) to the left and right of the centre apple. Secure the remaining apples over the spaghetti as before.

B

Tip
When making more than one of anything, it is always easier to roll out the required number of balls at the same time, to make sure they are all of equal size.

Tip
When cutting out sugarpaste with a shaped cutter, it is easier to release the paste from the shape if you dust it with icing (confectioners') sugar or cornflour first.

The shamrocks

1 Take off 30g (1oz) of the remaining bright green sugarpaste, and cut out four shamrocks using the shaped cutter (**B**). If you do not have a shamrock cutter, you can make them by hand by rolling three balls of the same size, and then rolling the balls into small cone shapes (**B**).

2 Flatten the cones and make them into heart shapes using tool No.4 (alternatively you can use a small heart-shaped cutter). Mark a line down the centre of each heart and on either side. Place the three points together and then roll a short stalk and attach to the base (**B**). Attach a completed shamrock in between each apple around the side of the cake.

Good Luck

The fence

1 Roll out 130g (4½oz) of mid-brown sugarpaste in between 1cm (⅜in) spacing rods. Cut out seven strips measuring 8 x 1.5cm (3⅛ x ½in) to make the posts. Cut one strip into three pieces, each measuring 2 x 1.5cm (¾ x ½in). Place these short pieces in between the four posts and secure with edible glue. Make a diagonal cut at the top of the remaining two strips and attach them at each end of the fence (**C**).

2 Push a short piece of dry spaghetti into the base of each strip leaving 2cm (¾in) showing. Using tool No.4, mark each post to look like wood and then, using a mixture of brown and yellow liquid food colour, paint on the markings (**C**). Position the fence to the back of the cake pushing the spaghetti into the top of the cake. Secure with edible glue.

Tip
To make cutting out in straight lines easier, use a marzipan knife or a pizza cutter.

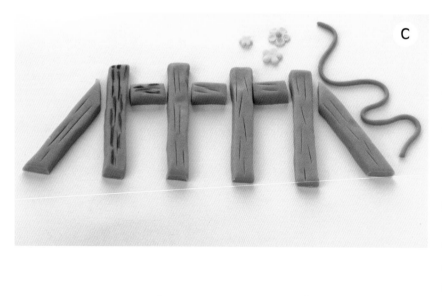

C

3 To make the grass around the base of the fence, soften 35g (1¼oz) of the remaining bright green sugarpaste with white vegetable fat (shortening). Fill the cup of a sugar press (or garlic press) and extrude short strands. Apply some edible glue around the base of the fence and attach the grass to give added support to the fence.

4 Roll a thin lace of the bright green sugarpaste (**C**) and intertwine it around the fence like a vine and then add some leaves.

5 Make some flowers using 20g (¾oz) of yellow sugarpaste. Using 1cm (⅜in) and 8mm (¼in) blossom cutters, press out the flowers and then open out the petals using the end of your paintbrush. Add a small ball of orange sugarpaste into the centre of each flower to finish (**C**).

6 Attach some flowers to the vine decoration on the fence. Arrange a few more flowers below the fence, and set a few aside for later.

Good Luck

The pony

1 To complete the pony, mix together 130g (4½oz) of brown sugarpaste with 20g (¾oz) of mid-brown sugarpaste to create a marbled effect.

2 For the body, take off 55g (2oz), roll it into a cone shape and place on to a cake card (**D**). Make the longest back leg by rolling out 18g (¾oz) into a sausage shape. Narrow above the hoof area and bend and shape (**D**). Push a short piece of dry spaghetti into the thigh area of the pony, apply a little edible glue and slip the leg over the top of the spaghetti.

3 For the shorter back leg, roll 7g (¼oz) into a fat cone shape (**D**). Push the pointed end under the body of the pony.

D

4 To make the tail, use 15g (½oz) of plain brown sugarpaste. Make a fat cone shape and mark the hair with the rounded end of tool No.4 (**D**). Push a short piece of dry spaghetti into the back of the horse, and glue the tail into place, curving it around the hindquarters of the pony.

5 Make the neck by rolling 20g (¾oz) of the marbled brown sugarpaste into an oval shape approximately 4 x 2cm (1½ x ¾in) (**D**). Push a piece of dry spaghetti into the top of the body. Apply some edible glue to one end of the neck, and slip over the spaghetti. Smooth the neck at the base with your finger to blend it in with the body. Leave 2cm (¾in) of spaghetti showing at the top to support the head.

6 For the front legs, roll 18g (¾oz) into a sausage shape, and narrow above the hoof and knee area, then shape the leg (**D**). Push a short piece of dry spaghetti into either side of the body, and slip the legs over, securing with edible glue. Arrange the legs into a natural position.

Good Luck

75

7 For the head, take off 28g (1oz) and roll into an oval shape then narrow around the bridge of the nose. Cut off the end of the muzzle (**E**). Replace this with another muzzle made from 4g (⅛oz) of mid-brown sugarpaste rolled into an oval shape. Attach to the head with edible glue.

8 For the nose and mouth, use the end of your paintbrush, make the holes for the nostrils. Take a small round cutter and mark the mouth (**E**). Add a small, flattened oval shape in white over the bridge of the nose (**E**).

9 For the eyes, roll two small cone shapes in white sugarpaste for the eyes (**E**) and attach to each side of the head. Make a small hole inside each white cone and add a tiny ball of black sugarpaste (**E**). Roll two small eyelids shaped like bananas in marbled brown (**E**) and glue over the eyes. Highlight the eyes with a cocktail stick or toothpick dipped into white paste food colour and use confectioners' glaze to make them shine.

10 For the ears, make two small cone shapes using 3g (⅛oz) equally divided. Make a straight cut at the base of each cone (**E**). Attach in an upright position to either side of the head. Secure the ears with tool No.1.

11 Attach the head over the spaghetti at the neck and secure with edible glue in the correct position, as shown.

The mane . . . .

1 Soften 14g (½oz) of brown sugarpaste with some white vegetable fat (shortening) and fill the cup of a sugar press (or garlic press). Extrude the lengths of hair for the mane (**E**) and secure with edible glue to the crest of the pony. The mane should fall to one side only.

2 Add a fringe to the head by rolling 3g (⅛oz) of brown sugarpaste into a flattened cone shape. Using tool No.4, mark the cone with downward strokes to create the hair (**E**).

3 Attach the finished fringe in between the pony's ears, bringing it down towards the eyes.

The hooves

F

1 Make four hooves by dividing 8g (¼oz) of mid-brown sugarpaste equally into four. Roll into short sausage shapes and flatten with your finger. Shape each piece into an arched hoof (**F**), and then glue to the end of each foot. Smooth the hooves with your finger to blend them in with the legs.

2 Using the sugar press (or garlic press) again, extrude a few strands of brown hair over the top of each hoof (**F**). Secure the completed pony on top of the cake with edible glue.

The red squirrel

1 To complete the squirrel you will need 25g (⅞oz) of brown sugarpaste with some chestnut paste food colour added.

2 For the body, take off 8g (¼oz) and roll into a small cone shape then place on to a cake card (**G**). Push a piece of dry spaghetti down through the centre leaving 1cm (⅜in) showing at the top. Dust the front of the cone with white dust food colour on a dry brush.

3 To make the back legs, equally divide 6g (¼oz) of the sugarpaste. Roll into a cone shape, keeping the narrowest end rounded. Reduce the thickness above the paw and bend to a sitting position (**G**). Attach the back legs to the body. Mark the paws with tool No.4.

4 To make the front legs, roll 2g (⅛oz) into a sausage shape. Make a diagonal cut in the centre (**G**). Mark the paws using tool No.4. Attach these to the body bringing the paws together and secure them with edible glue.

G

5 For the head, roll 4g (⅛oz) into a ball. Mark a line at the centre front using tool No.4. Add a small black ball for the nose on top of the line. Using tool No.5, make two small holes for the eyes on either side of the face. Fill the holes with two small black balls (**G**).

6 To make the ears, roll two small cone shapes and then flatten slightly. Make a straight cut at the widest end (**G**). Apply some edible glue to the head and secure the ears using tool No.1.

7 For the tail, roll 4g (⅛oz) into a flattened cone shape. Using tool No.4, mark the hair (**G**). Attach to the back of the squirrel in a curved shape. Place the completed squirrel on top of the cake. Add some extra grass and a few flowers to complete.

Good Luck

The horseshoes

1 Mix together 3g (⅛oz) of black sugarpaste with 13g (½oz) of white to make a grey shade. Roll out the sugarpaste and cut out three circles using a 2.5cm (1in) round cutter. Take out the middle of each circle with a 1cm (⅜in) round cutter (**H**).

2 Cut out a small piece from the top of each circle to form the horseshoe shapes. Soften the edges with your finger and mark the nails with some dry spaghetti (**H**).

3 Dust the horseshoes with silver lustre dust food colour. Glue one to the fence and the other two to the front of the cake.

The half-eaten apples

1 Roll 2g (⅛oz) of red sugarpaste into a ball. Take the small blossom cutter and take out a piece of the apple and set aside (**H**).

2 Add some white sugarpaste inside the cavity of the apple, and make a hole in the top. Add a small brown stalk to the top (**H**). Use the small piece you cut out of the apple and add a small amount of white sugarpaste on the top (**H**). Make two.

3 Place the finished apples and the bite-size pieces in front of the horse and add three small green leaves (**H**) to finish.

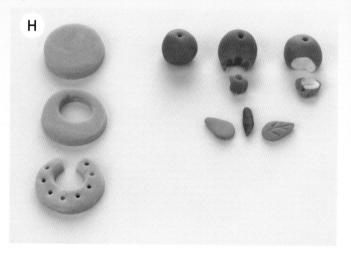

H

Good Luck

A Little More Fun!

Lucky Charms

Small cup cakes can be adorned with motifs from the main cake to further the good luck theme. Horseshoes, shamrocks and apples, made in exactly the same way as in the large cake, can be placed on top of white sugarpaste icing circles to make lovely treats for everyone involved.

Baby Bear's Christening

Baby bear has arrived safe and well, mother bear is proud as punch, and a magical fairy bear has come to grant the newborn a special wish as the little bears look on. The pastel colour combinations used for this cake make it suitable for a boy or a girl, and the lines are elegant, clean and simple.

"Bless you baby on your very special day"

You will need

Sugarpaste

★ 2kg 200g (4lb 13½oz) white
★ 300g (10½oz) yellow
★ 190g (6¾oz) pink
★ 125g (4½oz) pale blue
★ 110g (3⅞oz) mid-brown
★ 85g (3oz) peach
★ 2g (⅛oz) chocolate brown

Materials

★ 5cm (2in) round mini cake
★ 15cm (6in) petal-shaped cake
★ 25cm (10in) petal-shaped cake
★ Dust food colour in blue and silver lustre
★ Red food colour pen
★ Edible sparkle dust
★ Clear alcohol
★ Icing (confectioners') sugar or cornflour
★ 40g (1½oz) pastillage (see page 22)
★ 22g (¾oz) sugar flower paste (see page 23)
★ White vegetable fat (shortening)
★ Edible glue (see page 23)
★ Non-toxic glue

Equipment

★ 32cm (13in) petal-shaped cake drum
★ Silver florists' wire
★ Bead maker (optional)
★ 5cm (2in), 15cm (6in) and 25cm (10in) cake cards
★ 9cm (3½in), 6cm (2½in), 3cm (1¼in), 2.5cm (1in), 2cm (¾in), 1.5cm (½in) and 5mm (⅛in) round cutters
★ 3cm (1¼in) leaf cutter
★ Small star cutter
★ 4 cake dowels
★ Yellow ribbon 15mm (½in) wide x 115cm (45in) long
★ Basic tool kit (see pages 12–13)

Covering the board and cakes . . . .

1 To cover the cakes and the board, you will need 2kg 50g (4lbs 8oz) of white sugarpaste mixed together with 200g (7oz) of yellow sugarpaste to make a pale pastel yellow shade. Add more or less of the yellow to create the shade you prefer.

2 Cover the board in the usual way (see page 28) using 500g (1lb 1½oz) of pale yellow sugarpaste rolled out to an even thickness. Set aside to dry. Edge the board with the ribbon, securing it with non-toxic glue.

3 Place each cake on to a cake card of the same size and prepare them as required. For the 25cm (10in) cake, take off 1kg (2lbs 3¼oz) of the pale yellow sugarpaste, roll out to a thickness of 5mm (⅛in) and cover in the usual way (see pages 26–27). Set aside to dry, and then secure the cake to the centre of the cake board with strong edible glue.

4 To cover the 15cm (6in) cake, take off 600g (1lb 5oz) of the pale yellow sugarpaste and cover in the usual way. Set aside to dry.

5 To cover the mini cake for the top tier, use 150g (5¼oz) of the pale yellow sugarpaste. Dowel the cakes as described on page 29.

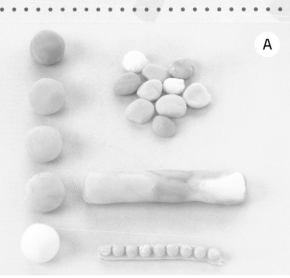

The bead trimmings

1 To make the bead trimmings you will need 25g (⅞oz) each of yellow, pink, peach, white and pale blue sugarpaste mixed randomly together (**A**). Be careful not to over knead the colours, as a random marbled effect is desired.

2 If you are using a bead maker, follow the instructions on the packet. Run a line of edible glue around the base of each cake to secure the bead trimming. You can roll the beads by hand if you do not have a bead maker; it is a little time consuming but worth the effort.

The roses and leaf decoration

1 Make two roses in yellow, two in pink and two in pale blue sugarpaste. Equally divide 16g (½oz) of each colour and roll into a thin sausage shape measuring 12cm (4¾in) long, then roll it out flat. Fold the strip over making a loose fold being very careful not to crack it (**B**).

2 Begin to roll the left end towards the centre until you have a rosebud the size you require. Cut off any remaining sugarpaste and squeeze the base of the rose in between your finger and thumb, thinning it down, and then cut off at the base of the bud (**B**).

3 Mix together the same five colours as for the beads randomly to make up 35g (1¼oz) in total and then roll out. Cut out six leaves and pinch each leaf at the base to shape (**B**).

4 Attach three leaves and three roses to the left side of the 25cm (10in) cake and to the right side of the 15cm (6in) cake.

Tip

To prevent any cracking on the fold, first knead some white vegetable fat (shortening) into the sugarpaste to make it supple.

The baby carriage

1 Roll out the pastillage and cut out the pram shape using the template on the right. Smooth around the edges with your finger. Place on to a non-stick surface dusted with icing (confectioners') sugar or cornflour. Using tool No.12, add the lines of stitch marks to the hood before the pastillage gets too hard (**C**).

2 Keep the finished shape very flat and leave to dry for 12 hours then turn the shape over to dry on the other side for a further 12 hours.

3 For the handle, roll a small sausage shape and curl it over (**C**). Keep flat and set aside to dry. When both pieces are completely dry, attach the handle to the carriage using strong glue made from the leftover pastillage mixed with edible glue to make a thick paste. Keep the pieces flat until the glue has dried.

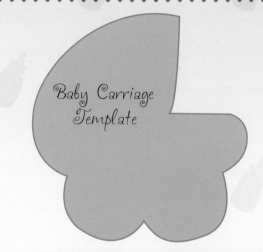

Baby Carriage Template

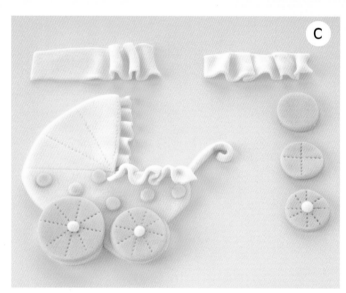

C

4 To make the wheels, roll out 20g (¾oz) of pale blue sugarpaste, and then cut out a 2.5cm (1in) circle for the back wheel, and a 2cm (¾in) circle for the front wheel (**C**). Using tool No.12, mark each wheel into four, and then into eight. Attach with edible glue to the baby carriage and add a small white round ball in the centre of each wheel (**C**).

5 Add some small circles to the side of the carriage using a 5mm (⅛in) round cutter and some blue and pink sugarpaste (**C**).

6 To make the frill on the hood and the top of the carriage, roll 10g (⅜oz) of white sugarpaste out into a thin strip. Frill with a frilling tool (or a cocktail stick/toothpick) and attach to the carriage using edible glue (**C**).

7 Place a small block of white sugarpaste on the centre of the top tier of the cake and secure with edible glue. Secure the completed baby carriage to the side of the block, and then push two lengths of dry spaghetti into the top and through the cake, giving support to the back of the carriage. Add some extra beads of marbled sugarpaste around the front.

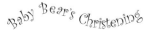

The balloons . . . .

1 To make three balloons you will need 5g (¼oz) each of peach, pink and pale blue sugarpaste rolled into three separate balls, and then flattened slightly.

2 Take a 6cm (2½in) length of florists' wire and dip the end into some edible glue, then push into the balloon. Roll a very small ball in the same colour and push this up the length of the wire and attach to the base of the balloon to prevent it from slipping down (**D**).

3 Make one balloon in each colour, then place them on a flat surface to dry.

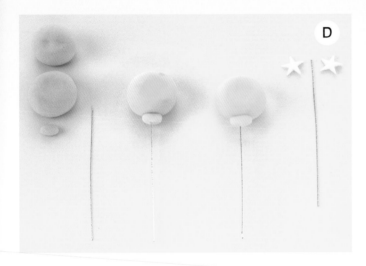

D

Tip
The wire on the balloon should be pushed into the teddy bear, and not into the cake. It should be removed before being eaten.

The wand . . . .

1 Roll out a small piece of sugar flower paste and then cut out three small stars using a small star cutter. Add some edible glue to one side of two stars, and then place a length of florists' wire in between two stars to make the wand (**D**). Press together to secure the wire and set aside to dry. Dust all three stars with silver lustre dust food colour.

The teddy bears

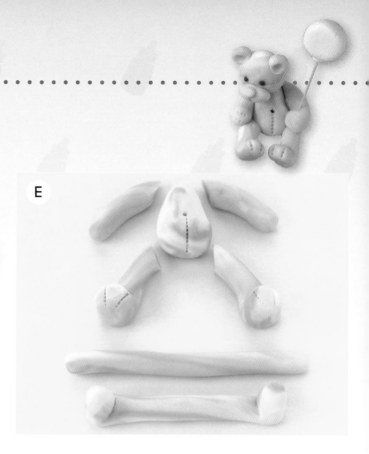

1 Mark out the edge of the 15cm (6in) cake into six equal sections with a straight pin. To complete the six teddy bears to go around the cake and the fairy bear, you will need 48g (1⅝oz) each of yellow, pink, peach, white and pale blue sugarpaste, making a total of 240g (8½oz) randomly mixed.

2 For the first body, take off 8g (¼oz) and roll into a cone shape (**E**). Place the cone on top of one of the points you have marked on the cake and push a piece of dry spaghetti down through the centre of the body and into the top of the cake, leaving 2cm (¾in) showing at the top.

3 For the legs, roll 8g (¼oz) into a sausage shape, turning up each end to form the foot. Make a straight cut in the centre, and then a diagonal cut at the top of each leg (**E**). Apply some edible glue and attach to the side of the body, arranging the legs over the edge of the cake.

4 Using tool No.12, press into the centre of the body to make stitch marks halfway up, and then add a navel with tool No.5 on top of the line. Add two lines of stitch marks on each foot (**E**).

5 For the arms, roll 6g (¼oz) into a sausage shape and make a diagonal cut in the centre (**E**). Attach to the top of the body.

E

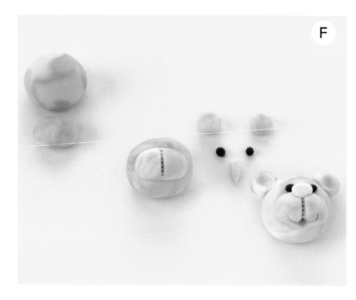

F

6 To make the head, roll 7g (¼oz) into a ball (**F**) and slip over the spaghetti at the top of the body.

7 For the muzzle, roll 2g (⅛oz) into an oval shape, and then attach to the centre of the face. Using tool No.12, mark a line down the centre (**F**).

8 To form the mouth and nose, make a smile on either side of the line using tool No.11. Insert tool No.5 in the centre of the smile and pull down slightly to open up the mouth. Make a hole at the top of the line and add a small cone shape for the nose (**F**).

9 For the eyes and ears, make two small holes just above and on either side of the nose. Fill each of the holes with a tiny ball of chocolate brown sugarpaste. Finally add two small balls for the ears. Attach with edible glue to each side of the head and indent them with tool No.1 (**F**).

10 Make five more teddy bears in the same way and place them evenly on the points you have marked around the cake. Give the three bears at the front of the cake a balloon to hold, pushing them carefully into the body at the desired angle.

The fairy bear

1 Add a little extra CMC (Tylose) to the paste you have left to complete the fairy bear, taking off 12g (½oz) for the body, rolled into a cone shape.

2 Make the legs using 12g (½oz) rolled into a sausage shape. Turn up at each end for the feet. Cut in half and push a short piece of dry spaghetti into the top of each leg. Apply a little edible glue and push into the base of the body and stand in an upright position.

3 Make the skirt by rolling out 10g (⅜oz) of sugar flower paste. Cut out a 3cm (1¼in) circle. Cut a 1.5cm (½in) circle out of the centre. Dust the work surface with icing (confectioners') sugar or cornflour and frill the edges of the circle with a frilling tool (or a cocktail stick/toothpick) (**G**).

4 Add a little edible glue around the waistline of the bear and slip the skirt over the body, easing it down around the waist. Lift the frills with the soft end of your paintbrush and allow to dry. Paint the edge of the skirt with blue dust food colour mixed with a little clear alcohol.

5 Make the arms as described for the teddy bears (opposite), using 7g (¼oz) of the marbled sugarpaste, and attach the left arm resting the paw on the edge of the frill. Set the right arm aside and keep it covered until needed.

6 Make the head as described opposite, using 10g (⅜oz) for the head and 2g (⅛oz) for the muzzle and place over the spaghetti at the top of the body. Omit the balls for the eyes, leaving these as holes only. The head should be turned in the direction of the mother and baby bear.

The fairy wings

1 Roll out 10g (⅜oz) of sugar flower paste very thinly. Cut out a 6cm (2½in) circle then divide the circle evenly into two pieces. Using tool No.4, mark out the shape of a wing (**G**). Then cut through the outline cleanly with a sharp knife. Turn the wing over and place it on the top of the other half circle. Cut around the outline of the wing to match (**G**). Soften the straight inside edge of the wing and curl it under.

2 Paint the wings with blue dust food colour mixed with a little clear alcohol. Using a clean brush, colour the pointed edges brushing from the tip inwards (**G**). Apply some silver lustre dust food colour in the same way. When the paint is dry, dust both wings with some edible sparkle dust. Apply some edible glue down the edge you have turned under, and attach to the back of the bear.

3 Stand the fairy bear on the cake board in the correct position and secure with edible glue. Attach the right arm to the body and rest it on the cake for support. Push the end of the wand into the hand of the fairy bear, and place a small ball of blue sugarpaste over the paw to secure the wire. Add the third star to the front of the fairy bear.

The mother bear

1 For the body, take 40g (1½oz) of pink sugarpaste and roll into a cone shape (**H**). Place the cone on to the top of the cake and push a piece of dry spaghetti through the centre, leaving 2cm (¾in) showing at the top. Push a small piece of dry spaghetti into the hip area ready to support the legs and at the top to support the arms.

2 Make the legs using 35g (1¼oz) of mid-brown sugarpaste rolled into a sausage shape. Turn up the ends to form the foot and make a straight cut in the centre. Mark the toes with stitch marks using tool No.12. Roll a small oval shape for the pad in pink sugarpaste and attach to the base of each foot (**H**).

3 Apply some edible glue to the top of each leg and slip over the dry spaghetti at the side of the body. Arrange the legs over the side of the cake.

4 For the skirt, roll out 35g (1¼oz) of pink sugarpaste into a strip measuring 20 x 5cm (8 x 2in). Shape the piece into a curve. Turn in the sides to hide the raw edges, and gather loosely at the top to form folds. Push the end of your paintbrush under the folds to help shape them (**H**). Attach the skirt around the waist of the bear, keeping the curved shape, and bringing the sides around towards the back of the bear in a semi-circle.

5 To make the sleeves, equally divide 10g (⅜oz) of pink sugarpaste and roll into a ball (**H**). Push a short piece of dry spaghetti into the base of each ball.

6 Make the arms using 16g (½oz) of mid-brown sugarpaste rolled into a sausage shape. Make a straight cut in the centre and apply some edible glue to the top. Push the arm over the spaghetti in the sleeve (**H**). Attach the completed arm over the spaghetti at the top of the body. Bring the arms forward to rest on the legs of the bear but do not glue them.

7 Using a red food colour pen, draw a dot pattern on the sleeves and around the hem of the dress (**H**).

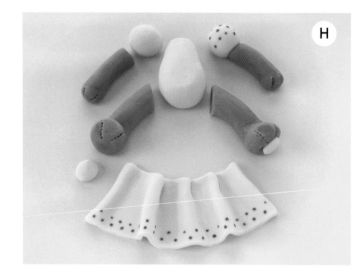

H

The mother's head

1 To make the head you will need 25g (⅞oz) of mid-brown sugarpaste rolled into a smooth ball. Place the ball over the spaghetti at the neck. Roll 6g (¼oz) into an oval shape and place this in the centre of the face, securing with edible glue. Mark a line down the centre using tool No.12 (**I**).

2 To make the nose and mouth, add a small chocolate brown cone shape on the top for the nose and mark the mouth at the base of the line by pushing in the end of your paintbrush (**I**).

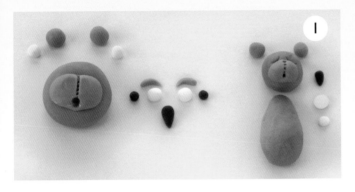

3 For the eyes, roll two small white balls (**I**) and attach them just above and on either side of the nose. Using a little chocolate brown sugarpaste, roll two much smaller balls for the pupils (**I**) and place on the top.

4 Make the eyelids from mid-brown sugarpaste rolled into banana shapes (**I**) and glue over the top of the eyes.

5 For the ears, make two small balls of mid-brown sugarpaste (**I**) and attach to the head. Roll a small ball of pink sugarpaste (**I**) and attach to the centre of each ear. Indent the ears with tool No.1. Position the head so that it is looking downwards at the baby.

The baby bear

1 To complete the baby you will need 22g (¾oz) of mid-brown sugarpaste. Take off 10g (⅜oz) and roll into a cone shape for the body (**I**). Push a short piece of dry spaghetti into the top.

2 To make the head, take off 8g (¼oz) and roll a ball for the head, slipping it over the spaghetti. To form the muzzle, take off 2g (⅛oz) and roll into a small oval shape. Mark down the centre using tool No.12 (**I**).

3 Make the nose, mouth, eyes and ears as follows. Add a small chocolate brown cone shape for the nose (**I**) and attach to the top of the face. For the mouth, push a hole into the base of the line with the end of your paintbrush. Mark the eyes with the small end of tool No.11 (**I**). Add two small mid-brown balls for the ears and indent with tool No.1 (**I**).

4 To make the dummy, roll a small ball of yellow sugarpaste and flatten with your finger (**I**), then attach over the mouth area using edible glue. Place a smaller ball of blue or pink sugarpaste (depending on the sex of the baby whose christening cake this is) over the centre (**I**).

The hat and shawl

1 For the hat, use 10g (⅜oz) of white sugarpaste, roll out and cut out a 3cm (1¼in) circle. Make a straight edge at the base of the circle (**J**). Apply some edible glue to the centre and place the baby's head on the top.

2 For the shawl you will need 40g (1½oz) of white sugarpaste. Roll out and cut out a circle using a 9cm (3½in) round cutter. Make a straight cut at the top, as you did for the hat. Apply some edible glue to the centre of the shawl and place the baby on the top. Wrap the shawl around the baby and secure the edges down with edible glue.

3 Place the baby's head over the left arm of the mother, and attach her right arm over the baby.

J

A Little More Fun!

Newborn Nibbles

These cute mini cakes can be made in fruit or sponge cake using the Silverwood multi-mini pan set (see Suppliers, page 126) and then covered in pastel-coloured sugarpaste. The pram, bears or roses and leaves from the main cake can then be used as decoration, with a line of beads around the base, to create the perfect take-home cakes for a baby shower or Christening party.

Best In Show

Just how did this mutt get top billing? He certainly has plenty of charm and personality, but his pedigree pals are not amused by the judges' decision, so they have decided to sample the cake first! This design would be the ideal choice for a doting dog owner, and you could even adapt the 'top dog' to look like their pooch.

"Delicious doggy treats all round!"

You will need

Sugarpaste

★ 600g (1lb 5oz) red
★ 400g (14oz) green
★ 195g (6⅞oz) white
★ 150g (5¼oz) black
★ 55g (2oz) brown
★ 40g (1½oz) mid-brown
★ 2g (⅟₁₆oz) peach

Materials

★ 15cm (6in) hexagonal cake
★ Paste food colour in red and yellow
★ Dust food colour in brown and silver lustre
★ Black liquid food colour
★ 7g (¼oz) sugar flower paste (see page 23)
★ Confectioners' glaze
★ White edible paint
★ Edible glue (see page 23)
★ Non-toxic glue

Equipment

★ 25cm (10in) hexagonal cake drum
★ FMM brick impression mat
★ 3cm (1¼in), 2cm (¾in), 1.5cm (½in) and 1cm (⅜in) round cutters
★ 2.5cm (1in) and 1.5cm (½in) hexagonal cutters
★ Green ribbon 15mm (½in) wide x 1m (40in) long
★ Basic tool kit (see pages 12–13)

Covering the board and cake

1 To cover the board you will need 400g (14oz) of green sugarpaste rolled out to a 3mm (⅛in) thickness. Cover the board in the usual way (see page 28). Edge the board with the green ribbon, securing it with non-toxic glue.

2 To cover the cake, roll out 600g (1lb 5oz) of red sugarpaste to a 5mm (⅛in) thickness and cover in the usual way (see pages 26–27). Tuck in each corner of the cake first, trim the edges neatly and finish by trimming the base of the cake with a marzipan knife. Save any leftover sugarpaste for use later.

3 Make a hole in the side of the cake using a 3cm (1¼in) round cutter. Using tool No.4, make the edges of the hole rough, as if the dog has taken a bite or two. Remove the red crumbs and save.

4 Attach the cake to the centre of the board with strong edible glue. Glue some of the red crumbs on to the board under the hole in the cake.

The brick wall

1 Mix together 130g (4½oz) of white sugarpaste with 30g (1oz) of mid-brown sugarpaste to make a cream shade. Roll out 100g (3½oz) of the paste to an even 3mm (⅛in) thickness. Place the brick impression mat over the top of the paste and press firmly and evenly into the paste, then remove the mat.

2 Cut the bricks into a strip the length of the mat by two bricks high – this measurement will be 14 x 2cm (5½ x ¾in). Continue to re-roll the paste, marking with the impression mat until you have enough bricks, interlocking them by removing the half bricks (**A**).

3 Dust the bricks with brown dust food colour and a dry brush (**A**). Attach the first part of the wall to the left of the hole in the cake, and continue the wall all the way around the cake ending it on the right side of the hole.

4 Add two more bricks to the centre of each section of wall. Cut out four individual bricks and set aside (**A**).

5 **Make some crumbs** to fill the hole in the cake with some of the sugarpaste left over from the wall. Attach the crumbs inside the hole with edible glue, and then prick all over with tool No.5. Set aside any leftover cream sugarpaste to make the bone, food bowl and the Pekinese dog later.

The mutt

1 **To complete this dog** you will need 100g (3½oz) of black sugarpaste and 29g (1oz) of white sugarpaste.

2 **For the body**, take off 57g (2oz) of black sugarpaste and roll into a tall cone shape; the height should be 7cm (2¾in) (**B**, see overleaf). Make a small hollow in the back, but keep the cone very upright.

3 Push a piece of dry spaghetti down through the centre of the body, leaving 2cm (¾in) showing at the top. Push a short piece of dry spaghetti into the side of the dog where you are going to place the back legs.

4 **To make the back legs**, take off 12g (½oz) of white sugarpaste and divide equally. Roll into a cone shape, keeping the narrow end quite rounded for the paws (**B**). Bend the leg to shape it into a natural sitting position.

5 Make the black fur covering on the legs using 1g (⅛oz) of black sugarpaste. Roll into a long irregular shape measuring around 3 x 1cm (1¼ x ⅜in). Create the ragged-edge effect by dragging tool No.12 outwards around the edges (**B**).

6 Apply some edible glue around the inside and top of the leg, and then apply the black fur. Smooth it gently around the shape of the leg. Attach the completed leg over the spaghetti on the body in a bent position. Using tool No.4, press gently to make the paw marks.

7 For the front legs, take off 12g (½oz) of white sugarpaste and roll into a sausage shape measuring 7cm (2¾in) long. Turn up the rounded ends to form the paw, and then make a straight cut in the centre. Turn the leg on to its side and, using tool No.4, make a diagonal cut down the back of the leg (**B**). Make the black fur covering on the front legs as described for the back legs.

8 Apply some edible glue and attach the legs to the front of the body. Mark the paws using tool No.4. Add some very small irregular shapes in black sugarpaste to the white parts of the front legs.

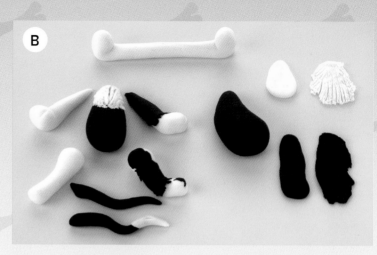

9 To make the chest fur, take 1g (⅛oz) of white sugarpaste and make a flat cone shape then roll it out thinly with your rolling pin. Take tool No.4 and drag it downwards to mark the fur. Make the edges ragged by dragging it around the edges (**B**). Attach to the top of the body to hide the top of the legs.

10 For the tail, roll 2g (⅛oz) of black sugarpaste into a pointed cone shape. Roll out 1g (⅛oz) of white sugarpaste and then cut out a 1.5cm (½in) circle. Apply some edible glue to the tip of the tail and wrap the circle around it (**B**).

11 Using tool No.4, mark the tip with downward strokes to look like fur. Make a diagonal cut at the top of the tail and attach to the back of the dog, curving the tail to give it movement.

The mutt's head

1 To complete the head you will need 34g (1⅛oz) of black sugarpaste. Take off 24g (⅞oz) and roll into a ball. Using your finger and thumb, gently roll and pull out the muzzle (**C**). Using tool No.4, make a line in the centre front of the muzzle.

2 To make the cheeks, take off 2g (⅛oz) of black sugarpaste and divide equally. Roll into two balls and place one on either side of the line, smoothing them to the side of the muzzle. Make some whisker marks on the front of each cheek by pressing tool No.5 into the sugarpaste to make small holes (**C**).

3 For the beard, randomly mix together a little white and black sugarpaste. Make a small cone shape and flatten with your finger. Using tool No.4, mark the shape with downward strokes to look like hair (**C**). Apply some edible glue to the base of the jaw and attach the beard.

4 To make the nose and tongue, take a small amount of peach sugarpaste and make into a small cone shape for the nose (**C**). Attach with edible glue to the top of the line. Roll a tiny sausage shape in peach for the tongue (**C**) and push this in between the beard and the base of the jaw below the line. Gently press the blade of tool No.4 into the centre of the tongue; this will secure it in place (**C**).

5 For the eyes, take off a little white sugarpaste and cut out a 1cm (⅜in) circle. Make the edges of the circle ragged using the same technique as before (**C**). Attach to the face where the left eye is to be placed.

Tip

When you roll the balls for the eyes, do not make them too big, because when you place them on to the face and flatten them, they become much bigger.

C

6 Using the end of your paintbrush, indent two small holes, one in the centre of the ragged white circle for the left eye, and one directly on to the face for the right eye (**C**). Using some brown sugarpaste, make two tiny balls and glue into the holes. Roll two much smaller balls in black and glue over the top. Press lightly with your finger.

7 For the eyebrows, make one small cone shape in black and one in white. Mark the cones with tool No.4, keeping the strokes going outwards the way the hair would actually lie (**C**). Apply some edible glue above each eye and attach the black eyebrow on the right and white on the left.

8 For the ears, take off 5g (¼oz) of black sugarpaste and divide equally. Roll into a cone shape and flatten the widest end with your finger (**C**). On the left ear add a small white ragged shape.

9 Add some glue to either side of the head and attach the ear keeping it upright. Use tool No.1 to press the narrow end into the head, and then gently fold the right ear forwards and keep the left ear cocked. Add a tiny ragged piece of white in between the ears on the top of the head.

10 Paint lightly around the right eye with white edible paint to lighten it and add a white dot to each eye. Paint the eyes with confectioners' glaze to make them shine.

11 Put some edible glue on the base of the dog and position him in the centre of the cake.

The rosette and the large bone

1 For the rosette, colour 6g (¼oz) of sugar flower paste with red paste food colour, and 1g (⅛oz) of sugar flower paste with yellow paste food colour. Take off 5g (¼oz) of the red flower paste and set the rest aside. Cut out a 2cm (¾in) circle and a 1.5cm (½in) circle in red sugar flower paste, and a 1cm (⅜in) circle in yellow sugar flower paste (**D**).

2 Using a frilling tool (or a cocktail stick/toothpick), frill around the edges of the red circles. Place the small circle on top of the larger one and attach with edible glue. Place the yellow circle on the top in the centre (**D**).

3 Cut a strip from the remaining red sugar flower paste measuring 6cm x 4mm (2⅜ x ⅛in). Fold in half, and then make a diagonal cut at each end. Attach this to the back of the rosette (**D**). Apply some edible glue to the mutt and place the rosette over making sure it is in good contact with the body.

4 For the large bone, roll 6g (¼oz) of cream sugarpaste left over from making the wall into a ball, and then into a sausage shape. Narrow the centre of the bone with your finger, leaving the ends nicely rounded. Using tool No.4, press into each end of the shape, marking it with a vertical line (**D**). Attach to the top of the cake beside the mutt.

The trophy and the small bone

1 For the trophy, roll out 13g (½oz) of brown sugarpaste to a 1cm (⅜in) thickness. Cut out one 2.5cm (1in) and one 1.5cm (½in) hexagonal shape (**E**). Attach the small shape on the top of the large one and secure with edible glue.

2 To complete the rest of the trophy you will need 4g (⅛oz) of white sugarpaste with a tiny amount of black added to make a pale grey shade. Take off 1g (⅛oz) and roll a small sausage shape measuring 2.5cm (1in) long. Push a piece of dry spaghetti through the centre leaving 5mm (⅛in) showing at the top and 1.5cm (½in) at the bottom (**E**). Push the end of the spaghetti into the base and secure with edible glue.

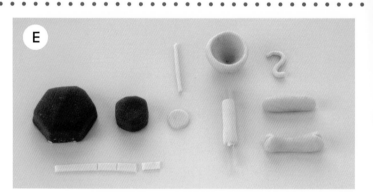

3 Roll 3g (⅛oz) into a ball and insert the end of tool No.3 in to the centre to hollow it out (**E**). Slip over the spaghetti.

4 To make the handles, roll a small amount of the grey sugarpaste into two thin laces and make an 'S' shape (**E**). Attach to the side of the cup.

5 For the name plates, roll out the remaining grey sugarpaste into a very thin strip and cut into six small rectangles (**E**). Set aside to dry, and then dust with some silver lustre dust food colour and a dry brush. Glue one name plate to each side of the trophy base.

6 Add a small bone inside the cup, made in the same way as the large bone, but using just 1g (⅛oz) of cream sugarpaste.

Tip

If you haven't got hexagonal cutters, you can use round ones for the trophy instead.

The food bowls

1 To create the bowl of biscuits, roll 6g (¼oz) of mid-brown sugarpaste into a ball and then flatten the top with your finger. Using tool No.5, press into the centre of the shape to hollow out. Using your finger and thumb, work around the sides to make them straighter (**F**).

2 Make the dog biscuits by rolling 1g (⅛oz) each of black, white and leftover red and cream sugarpaste into small sausage shapes. Cut each one up into small pieces (**F**). Apply some edible glue inside the bowl and fill with the biscuits.

3 Make the bowl with the sausage as for the bowl of biscuits, using 3g (⅛oz) of the leftover cream sugarpaste. Roll 1g (⅛oz) of mid-brown sugarpaste into a small sausage shape and attach to the inside of the bowl. Paint the sausage with confectioners' glaze to make it shine, then set aside.

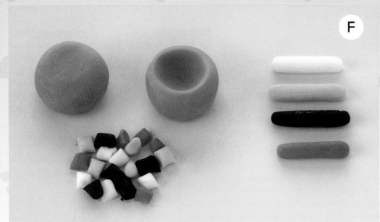

F

The Pekinese

1 To complete this dog you will need 42g (1½oz) of the leftover cream sugarpaste. Take off 30g (1oz) and roll into a cone shape for the body. Stand the cone upright and pull out a short tail at the back. Push a piece of dry spaghetti down through the body, leaving 2cm (¾in) showing at the top to take the head. Using the rounded end of tool No.4, mark lines on the body to look like fur (**G**, see overleaf).

2 To make the four paws, divide 2g (⅛oz) of cream sugarpaste into four and roll into balls. Mark the paws like fur using tool No.4 in downward strokes (**G**). Push short pieces of dry spaghetti into the front of the body, and secure the paws in a begging position with edible glue.

3 For the head, roll 6g (¼oz) of cream sugarpaste into a ball. Attach the head to the top of the body. Make a smile in the mouth area using the large end of tool No.11 (**G**). Using the soft end of your paintbrush open the centre of the mouth so that a small tongue can be inserted.

4 For the cheeks, take 2g (⅛oz) of black sugarpaste equally divided, make two small cone shapes and flatten with your finger. Using tool No.4, mark with downward strokes to give the appearance of hair (**G**). Attach on either side of the face curving them around the side of the mouth area. Add a small black ball (**G**) on the top for the nose.

5 For the eyes, roll two small balls of white sugarpaste (**G**) and attach just above and on either side of the nose. Add a tiny ball of black sugarpaste (**G**) for the pupil to each eye. The eyes should be looking in an upward direction.

6 Add the eyebrows using 1g (⅛oz) of cream sugarpaste equally divided. Roll into cone shapes and mark with tool No.4 (**G**). Curve them around the eyes and secure with edible glue.

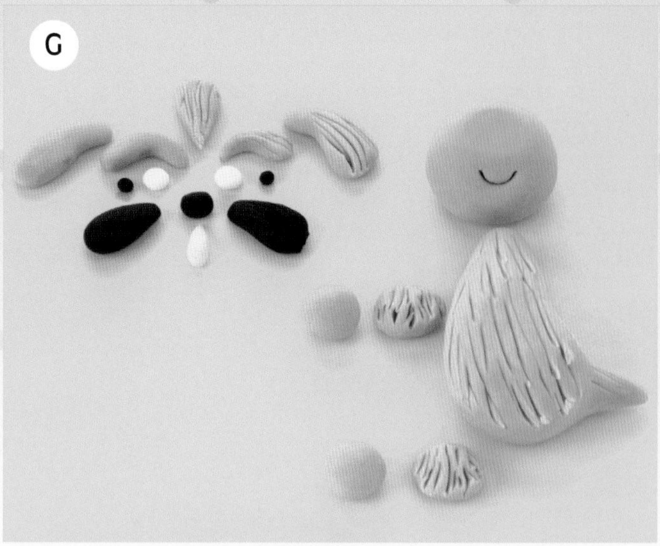

7 For the ears, make two more cone shapes using 2g (⅛oz) of cream sugarpaste equally divided, mark the fur as before (**G**) and attach to each side of the head. Roll another cone shape using 1g (⅛oz) of cream sugarpaste (**G**) and attach this in between the eyebrows taking it over the top of the head. Dust the ears with a little brown dust food colour.

8 For the tongue, roll a small cone shape in peach sugarpaste (**G**) and insert it inside the mouth.

9 Paint the eyes and the nose with confectioners' glaze. Attach the dog to the board, set back from the hole in the cake. Add a few red crumbs to his tongue and paws.

The Dalmatian

1 To complete this dog you will need 30g (1oz) of white sugarpaste and 2g (⅛oz) of black sugarpaste. Take off 13g (½oz) of white sugarpaste and roll into a cone shape for the body. Pull the tail out at the back keeping it straight. Push the back end of the body up into the air, making the back very curved (**H**). Support with foam until dry.

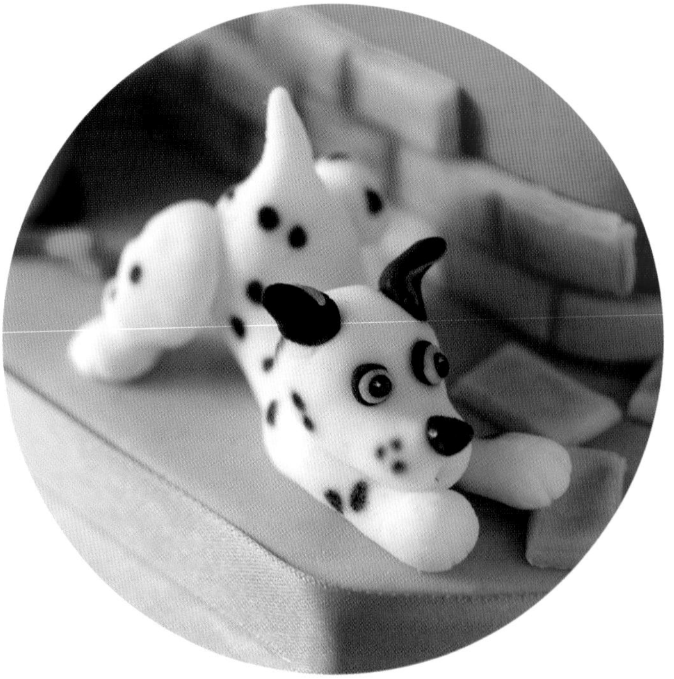

2 Make two back legs using 6g (¼oz) of white sugarpaste equally divided. Make a cone shape keeping the narrow end rounded for the paw. Thin out the ankle area by rolling it between your fingers. Bend the leg behind the knee and turn out the foot (**H**). Push a piece of dry spaghetti into the hip and attach the leg. Mark the paws using tool No.4.

3 For the front legs, take off 4g (⅛oz) of white sugarpaste and roll into a sausage shape, making a diagonal cut in the centre (**H**). Attach to the upper body on either side keeping them in a straight position, and then once again mark the paws with tool No.4.

4 For the head, roll 6g (¼oz) into a soft cone shape for the head, flatten the front of the snout slightly (**H**). Mark a vertical line at the centre front and then add a small black cone for the nose (**H**) at the top of the line.

5 To make the eyes, roll two small black balls (**H**) and attach to the head. Add two smaller white balls (**H**) over the top and press on lightly. Finally add two very small black pupils (**H**).

6 For the ears, take 1g (⅛oz) of black sugarpaste and divide equally. Make two small cone shapes and flatten slightly, then make a straight cut at the widest end (**H**). Using tool No.1, attach the ears firmly to the head.

7 Add some spots to the body, using a paintbrush and some black liquid food colour (**H**). Place the completed dog on to the board and secure with edible glue. Lift the left front paw and place a single brick underneath.

The Highland Terrier.

1 To complete this dog you will need 40g (1½oz) of black sugarpaste. Take 30g (1oz) and roll into a short sausage shape. Mark a diagonal line at each end of the sausage shape; this will divide it into two sections.

2 Pull out two short legs on either side of the line at both ends of the sausage. Mould the legs between your finger and thumb. Pull out the tail from the top keeping it short and erect (**I**). Use the round end of tool No.4 to mark the fur. Push a piece of dry spaghetti into the neck area.

3 For the head, take off 6g (¼oz) and roll into a cone shape. Flatten the pointed end of the cone and mark a diagonal line down the centre front (**I**).

4 For the mouth, use tool No.11 to make a smile directly underneath the line. Open slightly with the soft end of your paintbrush.

5 For the tongue, push in a very small cone shape made from peach sugarpaste and mark a line down the centre using tool No.4.

6 For the cheeks, make two small cone shapes using 1g (⅛oz) of black sugarpaste equally divided. Flatten with your finger and mark with tool No.4 to look like fur (**I**). Attach the narrow ends of the cones to the centre top of the snout and bring down around either side of the snout.

7 For the nose, roll a small black cone shape (I) and attach to the top of the snout.

8 For the eyes, roll two small balls of white (I) and attach to the front of the head. Roll two smaller balls of brown sugarpaste (I) and glue these over the top, press them on lightly with your finger to flatten. Add two tiny black pupils (I) over the top, looking towards the top of the cake.

9 Make two eyebrows by rolling 1g (⅛oz) of black sugarpaste equally divided into small cone shapes. Mark with tool No.4 (I) and arch them over the top of the eyes.

10 For the ears, make two small black cone shapes and add a smaller cone shape of peach sugarpaste inside (I). Attach in a very upright position on the head, using tool No.1 to help secure them.

11 To make the collar and lead use 1g (⅛oz) of leftover red sugarpaste, roll out into a thin strip and wrap around the dog's neck, making a loop at the end (I).

12 Paint the eyes and nose with confectioners' glaze. Attach the completed dog to the board behind the Dalmatian. Attach the bowl with the sausage behind him.

The Dachshund.

1 To complete this dog you will need 40g (1½oz) of brown sugarpaste. Take off 30g (1oz) and shape the legs and tail in one piece, as for the Highland Terrier (see page 101). Make this tail slightly longer and curve it upwards.

2 Narrow the underside of the dog making an upward curve underneath the body and at the same time lengthening the body to make it slimmer (J). Push a short piece of dry spaghetti into the neck area. Mark the fur on the body using the rounded end of tool No.4.

3 For the head, take off 6g (¼oz) of brown sugarpaste and roll into a long cone shape (J). Mark a vertical line in the centre front of the snout.

4 For the mouth and nose, take a round cutter and push it into the front of the snout to form the mouth (J). Roll a cone of black sugarpaste for the nose (J) and attach to the end of the snout. Slip the head over the spaghetti at the neck and secure with edible glue.

5 Make the eyes as described for the Highland Terrier (see step 8 above), placing them quite high on the head. Make a small banana shape in brown sugarpaste for the eyebrows and curve them around the eyes.

6 For the ears, equally divide 1g (⅛oz) of brown sugarpaste and make them into flat cone shapes (J). Mark the fur using tool No.4 and attach in a downward position close to the head. Support the head and the body of the dog with foam until dry.

7 Paint the eyes and nose with confectioners' glaze to make them shine. Secure the completed dog to the cake board, behind the bowl with the sausage. This dog is looking away from the cake.

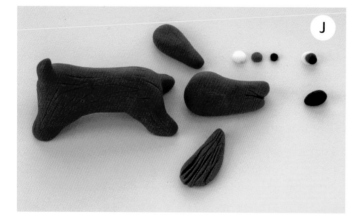

J

A Little More Fun!

Doggy Delights

The adorable pups on these mini cakes are made in exactly the same way as the main cake, but positioned so that they are looking over the top of the cakes towards their juicy bones. Cover the cakes in red sugarpaste and add a brick wall decoration around the bottom. Serve them on individual mini cake boards. Your guests are sure to sit up and beg for these!

Mother's Day Surprise

The little duck is showing her love and appreciation by bringing an unexpected gift on Mother's Day. A bumblebee has surprised her too! Baking this cake for a special Mum is just another way to say thank you for all she has done for you over the past year. It would also be suitable for a 'get well soon' or birthday cake.

"My Mummy's the best there can bee!"

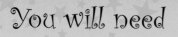

You will need

Sugarpaste

★ 750g (1lb 10½oz) white
★ 510g (1lb 2oz) yellow
★ 55g (2oz) mid-brown
★ 25g (⅞oz) pink
★ 15g (½oz) orange
★ 1g (⅛oz) black

Materials

★ Two 15 x 7.5cm (6 x 3in) cakes
★ Paste food colour in bright green, blue and dark green
★ Liquid food colour in black
★ Edible pink sparkle dust
★ 150g (5¼oz) sugar flower paste (see page 23)
★ Edible glue (see page 23)
★ Non-toxic glue

Equipment

★ 20cm (8in) cake drum
★ 15cm (6in) cake cards
★ 6cm (2½in), 5cm (2in), 4cm (1½in), 3cm (1¼in), 2cm (¾in), 1.5cm (½in), 1cm (⅜in) and 5mm (⅛in) round cutters
★ 1cm (⅜in) heart cutter
★ 1cm (⅜in) blossom cutter
★ 1.5cm (½in) square cutter (optional)
★ PME ribbed rolling pin
★ 2 flower stamens
★ Green and white spotted ribbon 15mm (½in) wide x 1m (40in) long
★ Basic tool kit (see pages 12–13)

Covering the board and cakes . . . .

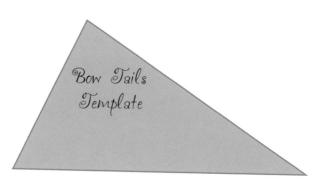

1 Colour 375g (13¼oz) of white sugarpaste with bright green paste food colour and then knead well until the colour is evenly dispersed.

2 Roll out the sugarpaste to a 3mm (⅛in) thickness and cover the board in the usual way (see page 28). Set aside any leftover sugarpaste for decoration. Edge the board with the spotted ribbon, securing it with non-toxic glue.

3 Place each cake on to a 15cm (6in) cake card. Prepare the cakes and then dowel them (see page 29).

4 To cover the stacked cakes you will need 500g (1lb 1½oz) of yellow sugarpaste. Roll out to a 5mm (⅛in) thickness and cover in the usual way (see pages 26–27), trimming the edges neatly with a marzipan knife. Set the cakes aside.

Tip

This is a tall cake (two cakes stacked together), so roll the paste out to a larger size than you need. This will allow the edges to fall on to the work surface, giving the sugarpaste some support and preventing stretching around the top while you are covering the cake.

Bow Tails Template

The bow around the cake

1 To complete the ribbon and bow you will need 140g (5oz) of white sugarpaste mixed with 145g (5⅛oz) of sugar flower paste. Knead together to make a smooth dough and then add some blue paste food colour. Continue to knead until the colour has been evenly dispersed.

2 Take off 125g (4½oz) and roll a strip measuring 34 x 2cm (13⅜ x ¾in) to go around the cake. Texture the surface with a ribbed rolling pin. Secure the ribbon to the cake approximately 3cm (1¼in) from the top. In order for the ribbon to be applied straight, measure from the top of the cake, marking a line with a straight pin. Make the join at the front in the centre.

3 To make the bow loops, take off 100g (3½oz) of the blue sugarpaste and roll out to a measurement of 34 x 5cm (13⅜ x 2in). Texture the ribbon with the ribbed rolling pin and cut in half.

4 Add some edible glue to the end of the strip and fold the other end over to make a loop. Turn the corner inwards and glue them into place (**A**). Roll some kitchen paper into a small sausage shape, and slip through the loop to keep its shape until dry. Repeat the process with the other bow loop. Set them aside to dry.

5 To make the tails for the bow, take off 50g (1¾oz) of blue sugarpaste and roll into a rectangular shape measuring 34 x 5cm (13⅜ x 2in). Roll over the surface with the ribbed rolling pin, and then re-cut to size if necessary (**A**). Cut out two tails using the template opposite and glue them into position at the front of the cake.

6 Attach the bow loops to the centre of the ribbon. Push a short piece of dry spaghetti into the narrow end of the loop to help secure it to the cake. Apply some edible glue to the back of the bow and press to the side of the cake. Support the bow underneath with some foam until dry.

7 To make the centre of the bow, use the remaining 10g (⅜oz) of blue sugarpaste and roll into a rectangular shape measuring 4.5 x 6cm (1¾ x 2½in). Texture with the ribbed rolling pin and then turn under the edges on the longest sides – be careful not to crease the paste when doing this (**A**). Push a piece of dry spaghetti into the cake and attach the centre of the bow. There should be no raw edges showing.

8 Attach the cake to the centre of the board with strong edible glue. Roll some small balls using 5g (¼oz) of white sugarpaste and glue them randomly around the cake – these will help disguise any slight unevenness.

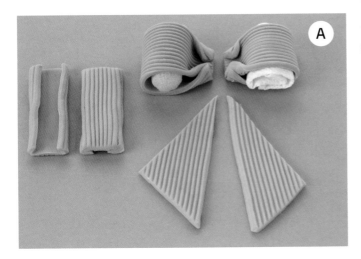

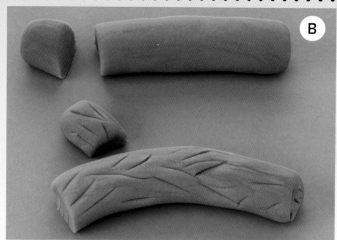

The log

1 **To make the log,** take 40g (1½oz) of mid-brown sugarpaste and roll into a sausage shape measuring 9cm (3½in) long (**B**).

2 Cut off 1.5cm (½in) from one end, and make a diagonal cut at the straight end (**B**), and then glue it behind the log to form a short branch.

3 Mark the whole log using the rounded end of tool No.4 (**B**). Place the log on to a 15cm (6in) cake card.

The mother duck

1 **For the body,** roll 40g (1½oz) of white sugarpaste into a tall cone shape. Pinch out the tail at the back of the cone (**C**).

2 Place the body on top of the log, and then push a piece of dry spaghetti through the body and into the log, leaving 3cm (1¼in) showing at the top.

3 **Make the legs** using 7g (¼oz) of orange sugarpaste equally divided. Roll into a cone shape and flatten at the widest end (**C**).

4 Using tool No.11, take out a half-moon shape on either side. Soften the edges with your finger and pull the points out slightly. Mark the foot using tool No.4 (**C**).

5 **Make the thighs** using 6g (¼oz) of white sugarpaste equally divided and rolled into two cone shapes (**C**). Push a short piece of dry spaghetti into the end of each cone, and then slip the legs over the top.

6 Attach the completed legs to the body on the log, securing with edible glue and turning the right foot in an upward position.

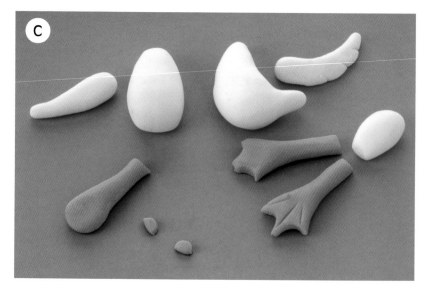

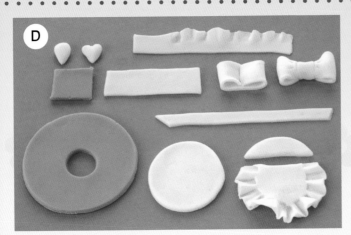

The skirt and bib

1 For the skirt, take 30g (1oz) of white sugarpaste and add some blue paste food colour. Knead well then take off 20g (¾oz) and put the rest aside for the hat. Roll out and cut out a 6cm (2½in) circle. Take out the centre of the circle with a 1.5cm (½in) round cutter (**D**). Slip the skirt over the top of the body and secure around the waist.

2 For the bib, cut out a 1.5cm (½in) square of blue sugarpaste and stitch mark around the edges using tool No.12 (**D**). Attach to the front of the body with edible glue.

3 Roll a tiny cone shape in white sugarpaste then, using tool No.4, indent the centre to make a heart shape (**D**). Attach to the front of the bib with edible glue.

The apron and the mother's wings

1 For the apron, cut out a 4cm (1½in) circle from 8g (¼oz) of white sugarpaste and frill the edges with a frilling tool (or a cocktail stick/toothpick). Cut off the top of the circle to make a straight edge (**D**). Glue the apron to the front of the skirt.

2 Roll out 14g (½oz) of white sugarpaste and cut a strip to go around the top of the apron and cross over at the back (**D**).

3 Make the bow from the same piece of paste by cutting out another strip measuring 1.5 x 4cm (½ x 1½in). Apply some edible glue to the centre of the strip, and then turn in the edges to make a loop, meeting in the centre. Turn the bow over and pinch the centre to narrow. Mark the bow with tool No.4 (**D**) and attach to the ties at the back of the apron.

4 Using 6g (¼oz) of white sugarpaste, roll out a thin strip measuring approximately 1 x 8cm (⅜ x 3⅛in) and frill the edge (**D**). Attach the frill around the duck's neck, securing it to the apron waistband.

5 For the wings, equally divide 16g (½oz) of white sugarpaste and roll into a tapered cone shape (**C**). Push a short piece of dry spaghetti into the shoulder area and attach the wings with edible glue. Bring them round to the front but do not attach the ends at this stage. Mark the feathers using tool No.4 (**C**).

The mother's head

1 To complete the head you will need 20g (¾oz) of white sugarpaste. Take off 18g (¾oz) and roll into cone shape for the head (**E**). Push a short piece of dry spaghetti into the centre of the face.

2 For the cheek feathers, take off 1g (⅛oz) and divide equally. Roll into a cone shape and, using tool No.4, make downward strokes to mark the feathers (**E**). Attach one on either side of the spaghetti.

3 For the beak, take 2g (⅛oz) of yellow sugarpaste and roll into a fat cone shape. Flatten the widest end to shape like a beak (**E**), and then attach it over the spaghetti securing with edible glue. Mark two short vertical lines at the top of the beak.

4 For the bottom of the beak, make a small banana shape in yellow (**E**) and attach it underneath. Roll a tiny cone shape in orange sugarpaste for the tongue (**E**) and attach it inside, marking the centre of the tongue with tool No.4.

> *Tip*
> *If you have a flower former, place the head inside to keep the shape while you are working on it.*

5 For the eyes, roll two small balls of white sugarpaste (**E**) and attach just above the cheeks. Using black sugarpaste, roll two more tiny balls for the pupils (**E**), attach to the top of the white eyes. Outline the eyes and add some eyelashes using a No.00 paintbrush and some black liquid food colour.

6 For the hair, make three very small tapered cone shapes and attach to the top of the head. The centre piece should be slightly longer than the pieces on either side (**E**).

The hat

1 Roll out 12g (½oz) of mid-brown sugarpaste and cut out a 4cm (1½in) circle. Make a straight edge at the base of the circle (**E**). Apply some edible glue around the head of the mother duck and attach the hat. Mould the brim into shape with your finger.

2 For the ribbon and bow you will need 10g (⅜oz) of the blue sugarpaste put aside earlier. Follow the instructions for making the bow of the apron on page 109 (**D** and **E**).

The flowers

1 Take some dark green paste food colour and mix it with a 2g (⅛oz) of the green sugarpaste left over from covering the board. Roll some thin laces to form the stems (**F**). Glue them across the front of the duck.

2 Cut out seven flowers from 2g (⅛oz) of pink sugarpaste using a 1cm (⅜in) blossom cutter. Open each petal using the end of your paintbrush. Paint the centre of each flower with some black liquid food colour (**F**). Arrange them over the stems. Save one flower to decorate the daughter duck's dress later on.

3 Bring the mother's wings forward as if holding the bouquet. Lift the completed duck on the log to the top of the cake and secure with edible glue.

The daughter duck

1 Construct the body as for the mother duck (see page 108), using 17g (½oz) of white sugarpaste for the body. Sit the cone into position on the top of the cake and then push a piece of dry spaghetti down through the centre, leaving 2cm (¾in) showing at the top.

2 Make the thighs using 6g (¼oz) of white sugarpaste rolled into cones, as described for the mother duck (see page 108).

3 Make the legs and feet as on page 108, using 7g (¼oz) of orange equally divided. Attach to the body and arrange on the cake, making one leg fall over the side.

The petticoat, dress and wings

1 For the petticoat, mix together 2g (⅛oz) of white sugarpaste with 2g (⅛oz) of sugar flower paste. Roll out and cut out a 3cm (1¼in) circle. Take out the centre using a 1.5cm (½in) round cutter. Frill the edge (**F**), and then slip it over the body.

2 Make the dress using 17g (½oz) of the green sugarpaste left over from covering the board. Roll out and cut a 4cm (1½in) circle. Frill the edge as on the petticoat, but do not make a hole in the centre (**F**). Apply some glue around the top of the duck and slip the dress over the body.

3 Make the wings using 14g (½oz) of white sugarpaste equally divided. Push a long piece of dry spaghetti through from the top, leaving 1cm (⅜in) showing, which is to be inserted into the right side of the body. This wing is outstretched and needs this extra support. Hold it in place with some foam until dry. Attach the right wing to the other side of the body, resting it on the dress.

4 Make a small collar using 2g (⅛oz) of white sugarpaste. Cut out a 2cm (¾in) circle and cut the circle in half (**F**). Attach to either side of the spaghetti at the neck.

The daughter's head

1 For the head, roll 16g (½oz) of white sugarpaste into a cone shape and slip it over the spaghetti at the top of the body. Push a short piece of spaghetti into the centre of the face.

2 Add two feathered cheeks as for the mother duck on page 110, using 2g (⅛oz) of white sugarpaste equally divided.

3 Make the beak using 2g (⅛oz) of yellow sugarpaste as described for the mother duck on page 110.

4 Add the eyes and outline with black liquid food colour as on page 110.

5 For the hair, roll three tiny cone shapes and attach to the top of the head as on page 110.

6 Make a bow using 3g (⅛oz) of pink sugarpaste rolled into a short sausage shape. Narrow in the centre and flatten each end with your finger then shape into a bow (**G**).

7 Using tool No.4, mark the centre of the bow with two vertical lines, and then mark three lines at each of the ends (**G**).

8 Push a short piece of dry spaghetti into the top of the head and secure the bow to this with edible glue. Glue the remaining flower in the centre of the collar.

G

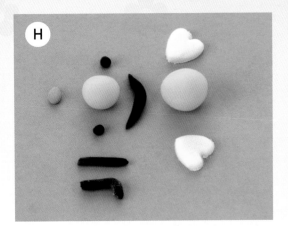

The bumblebee............

1 To complete the bee you will need 1g (⅛oz) of yellow sugarpaste, and half as much black sugarpaste. Take off two-thirds of the yellow sugarpaste and roll into a ball for the body (**H**). Push a short piece of dry spaghetti into the ball to support the head.

2 For the head, roll a ball from the remainder of the yellow sugarpaste (**H**) and attach over the spaghetti. Make a tiny banana shape using black sugarpaste (**H**) and place it over the top of the head bringing it around to the sides.

3 Paint on the stripes around the body using a No.00 paintbrush and some black liquid food colour.

4 Make a small nose using a tiny ball of orange sugarpaste (**H**). Attach to the centre of the face.

5 For the eyes, add two small black balls (**H**) and then paint on a smile using black liquid food colour.

6 For the wings, roll out 1g (⅛oz) of sugar flower paste, and then cut out two 1cm (⅜in) hearts (**H**). Attach to either side of the body. Push a small piece of dry spaghetti into the top of the daughter duck's wing, and then attach the bumblebee, securing with edible glue.

7 Make four tiny legs using black sugarpaste rolled into small sausage shapes. Turn each leg up at one end to form the feet (**H**) and glue to the body.

8 For the antennae, cut the top off two flower stamens and colour the ends with black liquid food colour. Carefully push them into the top of the bee's head.

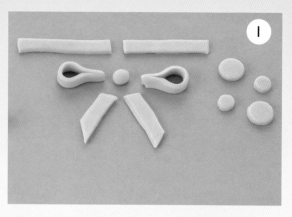

The present

1 For the box, take 25g (⅞oz) of white sugarpaste and shape into a square cube with your fingers.

2 To make the ribbons, roll out 15g (½oz) of pink sugarpaste, and then cut two narrow strips (**I**). Place them over the present and trim the edges neatly. Cut two short strips and make loops for the ties and attach them over the ties. Add a small round ball in the centre of the loops (**I**).

3 Decorate the present with some pink spots using the 1cm (⅜in) and 5mm (⅛in) round cutters (**I**). Finally, dust the decorations on the present and the duck's bow with edible pink sparkle dust.

A Little More Fun!

Yummy Mummies

These cute mini cakes continue the 'mumsie' theme. They are made using the Silverwood multi-mini pan set (see Suppliers, page 126), covered in yellow sugarpaste, wrapped with a blue ribbed band and then adorned with the present, flowers and bumblebee from the main cake. Why not make them for the other female members of your family – aunties, grannies and great grannies – so they don't feel left out?

Penguin Christmas

Wrapped up warm and revelling in the seasonal spirit, this family of carol-singing penguins makes a charming theme for a sumptous Christmas cake. Mum, Dad, baby and his siblings are all relatively quick and easy to make and will bring delight to young and old alike as the centrepiece of the festive table.

"I love to go a-carolling in the snow"

You will need

Sugarpaste

* ★ 1kg 300g (2lb 14oz) white
* ★ 200g (7oz) black
* ★ 30g (1oz) orange
* ★ 20g (¾oz) red
* ★ 16g (½oz) green
* ★ 1g (⅛oz) blue

Materials

* ★ 20cm (8in) round fruit cake
* ★ Dust food colour in pale blue and pink
* ★ White paste food colour
* ★ White vegetable fat (shortening)
* ★ Edible glue (see page 23)
* ★ Non-toxic glue

Equipment

* ★ 25cm (10in) round cake drum
* ★ 15cm (6in) cake cards
* ★ 1cm (⅜in) and 5mm (⅛in) round cutters
* ★ Small Christmas tree cutter
* ★ 1.5cm (½in) heart-shaped cutter
* ★ Blue ribbon 15mm (½in) wide x 1m (40in) long
* ★ Rice-textured rolling pin
* ★ Basic tool kit (see pages 12–13)

Covering the board and cake . . . .

1 Roll out 300g (10½oz) of white sugarpaste to an even 3mm (⅛in) thickness. When it is perfectly even, texture the surface using a rice-textured rolling pin.

2 Cover the board in the usual way (see page 28) and trim the edges neatly with a marzipan knife. Set aside to dry.

3 Cover the prepared cake with 600g (1lb 5oz) of white sugarpaste, rolled out to an even 5mm (⅛in) thickness. Using two cake smoothers, glide them over the top and around the sides to get a perfect and even finish. Trim the edges neatly with a marzipan knife.

4 Attach the cake to the centre of the board using strong edible glue. Edge the board with the blue ribbon, securing it with non-toxic glue.

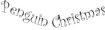

The frieze and trees

1 Roll out 250g (8¾oz) of white sugarpaste into a strip measuring 6 x 70cm (2½ x 27½in). Roll a rice-textured rolling pin over the surface.

2 Using a cutting wheel, shape the top into irregular peaks, making sure that the beginning and end of the strip match in height (**A**).

3 Apply some edible glue around the base of the cake and attach the frieze, making a neat join at the back. Allow the sugarpaste to dry before you carefully dust the cake and board with pale blue dust food colour.

4 Using the leftover white sugarpaste, cut out some trees using a small Christmas tree cutter (**A**). Vary the shapes of the trees in height, adding a tree trunk. Make a taller tree from a simple triangular shape (**A**).

5 Attach the trees in a group to cover the join at the back of the frieze and also to the front of the cake. Create a 3D effect with one of the trees by cutting out two trees, then cut the second tree down the centre and place half in the middle of the first tree at a 90-degree angle.

Tip

To make a perfect join in the frieze, overlap the two thicknesses and then cut through both. Remove the excess from the top and bottom layer and then press the edges together.

The mother penguin

1 To complete the mother penguin you will need 90g (3¼oz) of black sugarpaste. Take off 58g (2oz) and roll into a ball and then into a cone shape for the body. Pinch out a short pointed tail at the back (**B**, see overleaf). Place the cone in an upright position on top of a small cake card. Push a length of dry spaghetti through the centre leaving 2cm (¾in) showing at the top.

2 Make the feet using 12g (½oz) of orange sugarpaste equally divided. Make two cone shapes and flatten slightly, and then, using tool No.4, indent two claw marks at the front (**C**, see overleaf). Attach the feet to the base of the body.

3 For the front of the body, roll out 12g (½oz) of white sugarpaste to make a triangle shape the length of the body (**C**). Attach to the front of the penguin, folding the lower edge under to create an arched shape (**C**).

4 For the head, roll 20g (¾oz) of black sugarpaste into a ball and place inside a flower former. Using your paintbrush, indent across the centre of the face where the cheeks are to be attached (**D**).

5 To make the cheeks and beak you will need 2g (¾oz) of orange sugarpaste. Take off a small amount for the beak and set it aside. Roll the remainder into a short sausage and narrow it in the centre, keeping it fatter at each end (**D**).

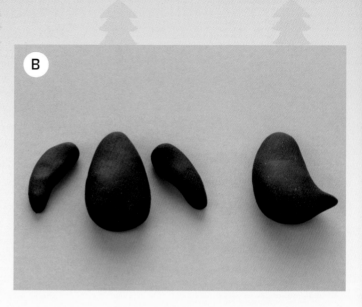

B

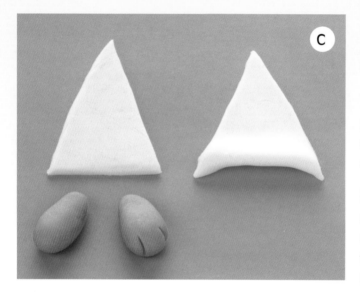

C

6 Apply edible glue across the centre of the face and attach the cheeks (**D**). Press the centre gently with your finger, and then push a short piece of dry spaghetti into the middle.

7 For the beak, roll a small sausage shape, making it pointed at both ends. Fold the shape in half lengthways and attach to the centre of the cheeks keeping the beak open (**D**).

8 For the eyes, cut out two 1cm (⅜in) circles in white sugarpaste and attach them on either side of the beak. Cut out two 5mm (⅛in) circles in blue sugarpaste and secure them on to the white circles using edible glue. Roll two tiny black balls for the pupils and glue these over the top of the blue circles (**D**).

9 Highlight the eyes using white paste food colour on the tip of a cocktail stick or toothpick, then blush the cheeks with pink dust food colour.

10 Apply edible glue around the neck and slip the head over the spaghetti.

11 To make the flippers, equally divide 12g (½oz) of black sugarpaste. Make a cone shape and flatten (**B**). Push a piece of spaghetti into the top of the body on either side. Apply edible glue and attach the flippers in a bent position.

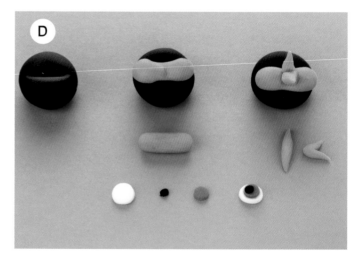

D

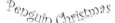

The green scarf and hat

1 For the scarf you will need 10g (⅜oz) of green sugarpaste, rolled out to measure 1 x 24cm (⅜ x 9½in). Fringe each end using tool No.4 (**E**). Wrap the scarf around the neck and secure with a little edible glue.

2 For the hat, take 6g (¼oz) of green sugarpaste and shape it into a pointed cone. Place the cone down on to the work surface to flatten it, and hollow out the inside using tool No.3 (**E**). Push dry spaghetti into the top of the head and apply some edible glue. Push the hat over the top of the spaghetti.

3 Make a band to go around the hat using 2g (⅛oz) of white sugarpaste rolled out into a strip measuring 1 x 9cm (⅜ x 3½in) (**E**).

4 Fill the cup of a sugar press (or garlic press) with 10g (⅜oz) of white sugarpaste softened with white vegetable fat (shortening). Extrude very short strands and attach them to the band then secure around the edge of the hat with edible glue. Add some tiny white balls to the green part of the hat for decoration (**E**).

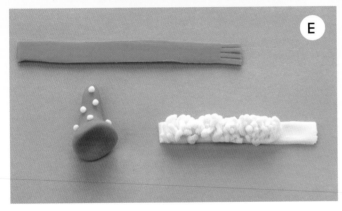

The book

1 Roll and cut out a rectangle for the cover measuring 1.5 x 3.5cm (½ x 1⅜in) using 2g (⅛oz) of red sugarpaste. Cut out two more slightly smaller rectangles using 2g (⅛oz) of white sugarpaste and attach them with edible glue in the centre of the book cover (**F**).

2 Bend the book in half and mark two lines for the spine using tool No.4 (**F**), then open out the book and arrange the pages so that they appear to be loose on the edges. Attach the book to the mother penguin's flippers securing with edible glue and support with foam until dry.

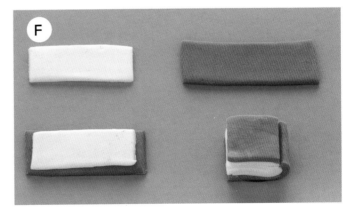

The hatching penguin

1 To complete all the baby penguins, mix together 7g (¼oz) of black sugarpaste with 70g (2½oz) of white to make a pale grey shade. Do not knead the paste too much as a marbled effect is desired.

2 To make the body of the hatching penguin, take off 6g (¼oz) and roll into a cone shape (**H**). Curve the cone so that the pointed end is at the back. Push a short piece of dry spaghetti into the rounded end to take the head. Apply some edible glue underneath the mother penguin and slip the body underneath.

3 To make the flippers, equally divide 1g (⅛oz) of grey sugarpaste. Make two small cone shapes (**G**) and attach to the side of the body in an uplifted position.

4 Make two small feet by equally dividing 1g (⅛oz) of black sugarpaste, and rolling two cone shapes. Flatten slightly and, using tool No.4, cut out two 'V' shapes in the centre of each foot to form three claws (**G**). Attach the feet underneath the body.

5 To make the head, roll 2g (⅛oz) of grey sugarpaste into a small ball (**G**). Apply some glue around the neck and slip the head over the top.

6 For the face, roll out 2g (⅛oz) of white sugarpaste and cut out a heart shape using a 1.5cm (½in) heart-shaped cutter (**H**). Attach to the front of the head with edible glue. Set the remainder aside for the cheeks. Push a short piece of dry spaghetti into the centre of the heart shape.

7 Mark the eyes with the end of your paintbrush, making two small holes. Roll two tiny balls of black sugarpaste (**H**) and place inside.

8 Make the beak using a small amount of orange sugarpaste rolled into a sausage shape with a point at each end, then folded in half (**H**). Push the beak over the spaghetti and secure with edible glue, keeping the beak open.

9 For the cheeks, add two small white balls (**H**) on either side of the beak. Dust the cheeks with pink dust food colour.

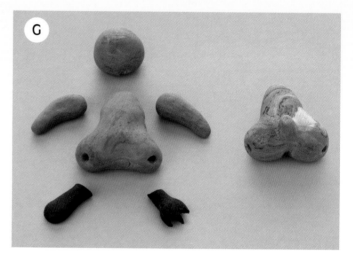

Tip

If you find it difficult to pick up tiny pieces such as the pupil, dip your brush into some edible glue and pick up the piece on the brush. This will allow you to place it into a small area where your fingers are too large.

The father penguin

1 Complete as for the mother penguin (see pages 119–121) using 90g (3¼oz) of black sugarpaste, 14g (½oz) of orange sugarpaste and 10g (⅜oz) of white sugarpaste. Make the white front smaller than the mother's.

2 Instead of a book, this penguin holds a song sheet made from 5g (¼oz) of white sugarpaste rolled out and cut to measure 4 x 3cm (1½ x 1¼in). Fold in the centre and attach to the end of the flippers. Support with foam until dry.

3 Make the red hat and scarf as for the green hat and scarf (see page 121), using 16g (½oz) of red sugarpaste. Instead of fringing the end of the scarf, press each end together and attach a ball of white sugarpaste (**H**).

4 Make the band around the hat using 3g (⅛oz) of white sugarpaste rolled into a strip measuring 1 x 10cm (⅜ x 4in) (**H**). Trim at the back to fit neatly.

The baby penguins

1 To complete each of the three baby penguins, take off 13g (½oz) of the grey sugarpaste and roll into a fat cone shape for the body.

2 Shape the leg area with your fingers and give each body a fat tummy, then pull out a small pointed tail at the back. Push the end of your paintbrush into the end of the leg (**G**). Stand the body upright and push a piece of dry spaghetti down through centre, leaving 1cm (⅜in) showing at the top.

3 To make the feet, equally divide 1g (⅛oz) of black sugarpaste and roll two small cone shapes. Make as described for the hatching penguin opposite (**G**). Apply some edible glue inside the holes at the end of the legs and insert the feet.

4 **For the head**, roll 6g (¼oz) of grey sugarpaste into a ball and slip it over the spaghetti at the neck.

5 **Make the face, eyes, beak and cheeks** as described for the hatching penguin on pages 122 and 123 (**H**).

6 **To make the flippers**, equally divide 2g (⅜oz) of grey sugarpaste and roll into flattened cone shapes (**G**). Push a piece of dry spaghetti into each side of the body and attach the flippers. Vary the positions of the flippers on each penguin for interest.

7 When dry, attach the two large penguins to the top of the cake securing firmly with edible glue. Place one of the baby penguins around the side of the father penguin and the remaining two at the front of the cake.

Penguin Christmas

A Little More Fun!

Festive Fancies

These fun and festive mini cakes can be made either from fruit cake or flavoured sponge. Cover the cakes with white sugarpaste and add a scaled-down version of the frieze from the main cake around the sides. The tops can be decorated with trees, woolly hats or penguin faces made in the same way as the main cake. They will make a refreshing change from mince pies and are a great way to make the main cake go further.

Suppliers

UK

Jane Asher Party Cakes
24 Cale Street, London SW3 3QU
+44 (0) 20 7584 6177
info@janeasher.com
www.jane-asher.co.uk
Sugarcraft supplies

Berisfords Ribbons
PO Box 2, Thomas Street,
Congleton, Cheshire CW12 1EF
+44 (0) 1260 274011
office@berisfords-ribbons.co.uk
www.berisfords-ribbons.co.uk
Ribbons – see website for stockists

The British Sugarcraft Guild
Wellington House, Messeter Place,
London SE9 5DP
+44 (0) 20 8859 6943
nationaloffice@bsguk.org
www.bsguk.org
*Exhibitions, courses,
members' benefits*

Ceefor Cakes
PO Box 443, Leighton Buzzard,
Bedfordshire LU7 1AJ
+44 (0) 1525 375237
info@ceeforcakes.co.uk
www.ceeforcakes.co.uk
*Cake and display boxes,
sugarcraft supplies*

The Craft Company
Unit 6/7 Queens Park, Queensway,
Leamington Spa CV31 3LH
+44 (0) 1926 888507
info@craftcompany.co.uk
www.craftcompany.co.uk
*Boxes, boards, decorations,
edibles, tools and ribbons*

Edible Art
1 Stanhope Close, Grange Estate,
Spennymoor, Co. Durham, DL 16 6LZ
Edible sparkles and dusts

Maisie Parrish
Maisie's World, 840 High Lane, Chell,
Stoke on Trent, Staffordshire ST6 6HG
+44 (0)1782 876090
maisie.parrish@ntlworld.com
www.maisieparrish.com
*Novelty cake decorating, one-to-
one tuition, workshops and demos*

Guy Paul & Co. Ltd
Unit 10 The Business Centre,
Corinium Industrial Estate,
Raans Road, Amersham,
Buckinghamshre HP6 6FB
+44 (0) 1494 432121
sales@guypaul.co.uk
www.guypaul.co.uk
Sugarcraft and bakery supplies

Pinch of Sugar
1256 Leek Road, Abbey Hulton,
Stoke on Trent ST2 8BP
+44 (0) 1782 570557
sales@pinchofsugar.co.uk
www.pinchofsugar.co.uk
*Bakeware, tools, boards and
boxes, sugarcraft supplies, ribbons,
colours, decorations and candles*

Renshaws
Crown Street, Liverpool L8 7RF
+44 (0) 870 870 6954
enquiries@renshaw-nbf.co.uk
www.renshaw-nbf.co.uk
*Caramels, Regalice sugarpastes,
marzipans and compounds*

Alan Silverwood Ltd
Ledsam House, Ledsam Street,
Birmingham B16 8DN
+44 (0) 121 454 3571
sales@alan-silverwood.co.uk
www.alansilverwood.co.uk
Bakeware, multi-mini cake pans

Squires Group
Squires House, 3 Waverley Lane,
Farnham, Surrey GU9 8BB
+44 (0) 1252 711749
info@squires-group.co.uk
www.squires-shop.com
*Bakeware, tools, boards, sugarcraft
supplies, ribbons, edible gold and
silver leaf, decorations and candles*

USA

All In One Bake Shop
8566 Research Blvd, Austin, TX 78758
+1 512 371 3401
info@allinonebakeshop.com
www.allinonebakeshop.com
*Cake making and
decorating supplies*

Beryl Cake Decorating Supplies
PO Box 1584 N. Springfield, VA 22151
+1 800 488 2749
beryls@beryls.com
www.beryls.com
*Cake decorating and
pastry supplies*

Caljava International School of
Cake Decorating and Sugar Craft
19519 Business Center Drive,
Northridge, CA 91324
+1 818 718 2707
criselda@caljavaonline.com
www.cakevisions.com
Flowers and other decorations

European Cake Gallery
844 North Crowley Road,
Crowley, TX 76036
+1 817 297 2240
info@thesugarart.com
www.europeancakegallery.us
www.thesugarart.com
Cake and sugarcraft supplies

Global Sugar Art
7 Plattsburgh Plaza,
Plattsburgh, NY 12901
+1 800 420 6088
info@globalsugarart.com
www.globalsugarart.com
Everything sugarcraft

Wilton School of Cake
Decorating and Confectionery Art
7511 Lemont Road, Darien, IL 60561
+1 630 985 6077
wiltonschool@wilton.com
www.wilton.com
*Bakeware and cake decorating
supplies, tuition*

BRAZIL

Boloarte
Rue Enes De Souza, 35 – Tijuca,
Rio De Janeiro RJ – CEP 20521 – 210
+55 (21) 2571 2242/2317 9231
cursos@boloarte.com.br
www.boloarte.com.br
*Cake decorating, sugarcraft
supplies and events*

NETHERLANDS

Planet Cake
Zuidplein 117, 3083 CN,
Rotterdam
+31 (0) 10 290 9130
info@cake.nl www.cake.nl
Cake making/decorating supplies

GERMANY

Staedter GambH
Am Kreuzweg 1 .D35469
Allendorf/Lda.
+ 49 6407 4034 1000
info@staedter.de
www.staedter.de
*Bakeware, tools, decorations
and accessories*

AUSTRALIA

Planet Cake
106 Beattie Street,
Balmain, NSW 2041
+61 (2) 9810 3843
info@planetcake.com.au
www.planetcake.com.au
*Cake making and
decorating supplies*

About the Author

*Maisie Parrish is often told she has magic hands, and when she begins
to work something magical does indeed happen …*

She began her career modelling salt dough, and steadily built up the UK's
most successful doughcraft company, with her characters selling in
department stores worldwide. A high point of this period was being asked
to create a new range for animation giant Walt Disney in Florida.

When she was approached to contribute to a well-known sugarcraft
magazine, she had to educate herself in the art of three-dimensional
figure modelling in sugar – and the next stage in her successful
career began. Being completely self-taught, Maisie's cute and
colourful characters have a unique quality that is instantly
recognizable and much copied.

People find it difficult to believe that she never actually bakes
cakes for anyone – she doesn't have time! As an accredited
demonstrator for the British Sugarcraft Guild, her days are
filled designing, teaching and demonstrating to others how
to decorate them. Her talent takes her around the world,
sometimes visiting three countries in a single month, and her
fans travel thousands of miles to visit her home studio for a
chance to learn from the master.

Maisie has enjoyed several television appearances, including *The Good
Food Show* and *QVC*, and she is the author of seven books, with more titles
in the pipeline. Further examples of her work can be seen on her website,
www.maisieparrish.com where she welcomes you into **Maisie's World**.

Acknowledgments

My grateful thanks go to Renshaws for supplying me with a wonderful range of their ready-made sugarpastes – with so many beautiful colours in their range, it has helped to make this book outstanding. Thanks also to Jennifer Fox-Proverbs, Charly Bailey and the team at David & Charles who have given me so much encouragement and professional help in the making of this book. A special thanks to Ame Verso who has done so much work on the editing side, and of course the photographers Karl Adamson and Simon Whitmore. Thanks also to Alan Culpitt for website design services, www.culpitt.co.uk.

Index